CONTROL
YOURSELF!

CONTROL YOURSELF!

Practicing the Art of Self-Discipline

/ D. G. KEHL /

 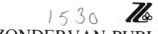
ZONDERVAN PUBLISHING HOUSE
of The Zondervan Corporation
GRAND RAPIDS, MICHIGAN

Lines from "Bearded Oaks," from *Selected Poems: 1923–1975*, by Robert Penn Warren, are reprinted by permission of Random House, Inc.

Lines from "The Heavy Bear Who Goes With Me," from *In Dreams Begin Responsibilities*, by Delmore Schwartz, copyright 1938 by New Directions, are reprinted by permission of New Directions Pub. Corp.

Lines from "Home Burial" and "Fire and Ice," from *The Poetry of Robert Frost*, ed. by Edward Connery Lathem, copyright 1923, 1930, 1939, © 1969 by Holt, Rinehart and Winston, copyright 1951, © 1958 by Robert Frost, © 1967 by Lesley Frost Ballentine, are reprinted by permission of Holt, Rinehart and Winston, Pub.

Special thanks for their suggestions and help in the preparation of the manuscript go to Judith Markham of Zondervan and to Fritz Ridenour.

Library of Congress Cataloging in Publication Data
Kehl, D. G.
 Control yourself

 1. Self-control. I. Title.
 BV4647 .S39K43   241'.4   81-21934
 ISBN 0-310-45001-2   AACR2

Unless otherwise indicated, Scripture is from The New International Version, copyright © 1978 by New York International Bible Society.

Edited by Evelyn Bence

Printed in the United State of America

83 84 85 86 87 88 — 10 9 8 7 6 5 4 3 2

To
the memory of my parents,
Harry and Annie Kehl,
from whom I first learned self-discipline,
and to
my wife, *Wanda,*
and my sons,
Kevin Lane
and
Kenyon Lee,
from whom I am still learning.

Contents

Foreword

Have you ever heard a message on the fruit of the Spirit? Sure
you have! What did it stress? The fruit of the Spirit is love?
Probably. But is that what the Scripture says? No! Rather, Scripture says, "But the fruit of the Spirit is love, joy, peace, patience,
kindness, goodness, faithfulness, gentleness, self-control . . ."
(Gal. 5:22–23). Notice that it does not say "the fruits of the
Spirit" but "the fruit of the Spirit." That is, there are not nine
fruits of the Spirit; there is a nine-fold fruit of the Spirit. In
essence, this nine-fold fruit of the Spirit is a portrayal of genuine
Christlikeness, and we are not to emphasize one dimension of it
apart from the others. Yet, how often have you heard a message
on "the fruit of the Spirit is self-control"? Isn't it interesting that
we tend to take the first dimension, love, and ignore the last
dimension, self-control? When this happens, love tends to degen-
erate into sentimentality rather than to be a demonstration of the
love which was characterized by Christ. Paul hits on this point
when he urges a disciplined love in these words to the Philippian
church: "And this I pray, that your love may abound still more
and more in real knowledge and all discernment, so that you may
approve the things that are excellent, in order to be sincere and
blameless until the day of Christ; having been filled with the fruit
of righteousness which comes through Jesus Christ, to the glory
and praise of God." In other words, love that is not accompanied
by self-control will be apart from "real knowledge and spiritual
discernment." It will find itself approving things that are not
excellent and being blamable at the day of Christ.

As I have read through this excellent treatment of the fruit of
the Spirit—self-control—I have had occasion to praise God
again and again. In the past I have read articles by Dr. Kehl such
as "Sneaky Stimuli and How to Resist Them," "The Two Ways
of Words," "The Devil's Electric Carrot," and others and have
been spiritually and practically edified every time. This book is

not unlike the many articles that he has written. It is a thoroughly scriptural and intelligent treatise that is at the same time intensely practical. It has already met several needs in my personal life, and I intend to keep it as a companion that I shall work through again and again in the years to come.

When I finished reading the manuscript, I could not but think of the words of Mordecai to Esther, "And who knows whether thou art come to the kingdom for such a time as this?" Surely there has been a great need for a systematic and practical treatment of this dimension of the fruit of the Spirit, and I believe that our God has brought Dr. Kehl to the fore to supply this urgent need for us. In a day when people have been taught to do whatever feels good to them, thus creating behavioral chaos, this work stands out as a bright light to lead us toward that goal of Christlikeness so that the reflection of Christ through us shall be with less and less distortion. "But we all, with unveiled face beholding as in a mirror the glory of the Lord, are being transformed into the same image from glory to glory, just as from the Lord, the spirit" (2 Cor. 3:18).

EARL D. RADMACHER
President
Western Conservative Baptist Seminary

Who Is in Control?

The eighty-seven passengers and crew aboard TWA Flight 841 had just finished eating and were settled back for the last leg of their flight from New York to Minneapolis. With the sophisticated Boeing 727 on autopilot, everything seemed routine, smooth, perfectly under control. Then, suddenly, at 39,000 feet over Flint, Michigan, the plane began to shake, veering sharply to the right and nosing downward into a barrel roll. Cabin fixtures shattered; objects flew through the air; people screamed. As the huge 727 plummeted 24,000 feet in less than a minute, the pilot struggled to regain control. In a desperate effort he lowered the landing gear, causing the plane to level off—perhaps two seconds before crashing! Following a hard but safe landing of the damaged plane at the Detroit Metropolitan Airport, officials called the plane's recovery from a 360-degree roll a "miracle."

How much like this sophisticated machine speeding out of control, nearly causing a major disaster, is a human life, designed by the Creator for harmonious order but running so out of control that nothing short of a miracle will bring recovery! Consider the multiplied tragedy of not one but scores, hundreds, even thousands of lives running blindly out of control toward certain disaster. Is your life one of those? Or are you under control? And if so, under *whose* control?

HOW CONTROLLED IS YOUR LIFE?

Take a few moments to assess the degree of self-control you manifested in the past week. Take the following self-discipline inventory, answering each question as honestly as you can.

	Yes	No

I. Devotional

1. Am I daily, continuously, being filled with the Spirit?
2. Do I have a definite time set aside each day for prayer and Bible study?
3. Do I regularly memorize Scripture and apply it daily to life's situations?
4. Do I make a regular, consistent effort to share my faith with others?
5. Am I steady and stable in my Christian life, experiencing daily victory rather than feeling victorious one day and defeated the next?

II. Mental

1. Do I consistently manifest the mind of Christ?
2. Does the daily renewal of my mind (Eph. 4:22–24) prevent my mind from growing dull and sluggish?
3. Does divine thought-control prevent my thoughts from wandering unrestrainedly into carnality?
4. Have I learned to meditate often upon spiritual things?
5. Is my mind steadfast? Is it seldom shaken or distracted by doubt, confusion, and mental turmoil?

III. Emotional

1. Have I learned to express positively the seven major emotions (love, sorrow, guilt, jealousy, fear, anger, hate), reacting to emotional stimuli in a God-pleasing way? ＿＿ ＿＿

2. Have I learned to surrender my "rights" to God? ＿＿ ＿＿

3. Do I manifest a "sweet reasonableness" toward all people? ＿＿ ＿＿

4. Have I learned not to allow trivial matters, such as personal affront and criticism, warranted or not, to upset me? ＿＿ ＿＿

5. Have I learned not to be easily discouraged or offended? ＿＿ ＿＿

IV. Physical

1. Do I glorify God through my body, the temple of His Spirit? ＿＿ ＿＿

2. Do I take care of my body, making sure it gets a balanced diet, sufficient exercise, proper rest, and medical attention? ＿＿ ＿＿

3. Do I master my body, putting it in subjection, so that it effectively serves the cause of Christ? ＿＿ ＿＿

4. Have I prevented fleshly appetites from becoming my god? ＿＿ ＿＿

5. Do I have consistent victory over gluttony, lust, and sloth? ＿＿ ＿＿

V. Verbal

1. Have I learned that my tongue is a forceful power for the cause of good? ＿＿ ＿＿

2. Is my tongue under control? ＿＿ ＿＿

3. Do I have a sanctified, rather than a foul, mouth? ＿＿ ＿＿

4. Have I learned to season my speech with the salt of grace?   _____ _____

5. Do the words I speak cause people to reverence God and put their trust in Him?   _____ _____

VI. Time

1. Do I feel a sense of urgency to "redeem" for His glory whatever time God gives me in this life?   _____ _____

2. Have I set and observed valid, God-pleasing priorities in my life?   _____ _____

3. Have I learned not to waste time through distraction and mismanagement?   _____ _____

4. Do I get things done on time, without procrastination?   _____ _____

5. Am I habitually on time for meetings and appointments?   _____ _____

Assess the results carefully. How many "yes" responses could you honestly check? Which areas seem to give you the most difficulty? Perhaps the following "key" will be of further help in your assessment:

Yes responses

26–30   Are you Michael the Archangel?

21–25   You are exceptional. Or did your halo slip down over your eyes?

16–20   Did you understand the questions? This book can help you improve and can give you insights into helping others become more self-disciplined.

11–15   Welcome to the growing crowd of people who realize their need of self-discipline.

6–10   Welcome to a larger crowd! God can use this book to improve your self-discipline.

1–5   Congratulations on your honesty! Read this book prayerfully; ask God to help you become more self-disciplined.

The above questions really are asking: Who was in control of your life during the past week? There are four possibilities or combinations thereof: (1) the fleshly self (the *sarcos* of the Scriptures); (2) the worldly system (the *cosmos*)—consisting of contemporary society and its distorted values, especially as reflected and conveyed by the mass media, other people, and everyday circumstances; (3) Satan (the *diabolos*); or (4) God, by His Spirit and His Word working through our faculties.

Most of us think we are in control—but are we really?

REACTIONS REVEAL CONTROL

Perhaps the best measure of who is in control is not action but spontaneous reaction. Suppose I'm walking down the street, and someone comes along and pushes me off the sidewalk into the gutter. My temper flares, and I angrily push him off the sidewalk, adding an abusive word or two. I've done to him what he did to me—and more. When we react the way others act toward us, *they* control us.

Remember that business meeting (maybe even a church meeting) when one person spoke harshly and bitterly, and then someone else responded in the same way? Harsh, bitter words beget harsh, bitter words. Actions are controlling reactions. Or maybe someone falsely accuses you, and then you respond in kind, allowing yourself to be controlled by that person. "Do not answer a fool according to his folly," Solomon said, "or you will be like him yourself" (Prov. 26:4).

How do you react when another driver tailgates for miles, then passes and cuts sharply in front of you, nearly causing a collision? Do you honk the horn, shake your fist, and mutter (not imprecations, but minced oaths)? If so, this stranger's reckless, thoughtless driving has controlled you, determining your behavior!

Recently, I was shocked by my own spontaneous reaction. After searching twenty minutes for a parking space, I spotted what appeared to be the only space for miles. As I moved toward it, a green Porsche dashed in before me. My initial reaction was to lose my cool. Only with God's help was I able to think, "Oh, well, maybe he's in a bigger hurry than I am."

Who or what controls your life at home? Do the attitudes, moods, or actions of your spouse control your reactions? If you allow the surliness or inconsiderateness of your spouse to make you surly and inconsiderate, then he or she controls you. Some parents' reactions are determined by their offsprings' actions. For if a parent responds to a child's angry words and raised voice with angry words and raised voice, he or she is being controlled by the child.

The Greek philosopher Epictetus said, "No man is free who is not master of himself." And no person is master of himself if he allows the actions of others to dictate his own reactions.

Regardless of how others act toward us, we have the power through God's Spirit to act and react in spiritual, and therefore free, ways. The apostle Paul wrote to the Corinthians: " 'Everything is permissible for me'—but not everything is beneficial. 'Everything is permissible for me'—but I will not be mastered by anything'' (1 Cor. 6:12).

Master of self and mastered by nothing—that is the ideal. But what *is* spiritual self-mastery or self-discipline, and how is it to be achieved in an age of little discipline and much self-indulgence? We often hear the expression, "Control yourself." Or, "Get hold of yourself." But how is self-control, self-restraint, to be achieved? To give such a command is somewhat like telling a young person to "go get educated."

SELF-DISCIPLINE IS OUT OF FASHION

Ours is most certainly an uncontrolled, undisciplined age—an age of self-indulgence. "If it feels good, do it," and "If it works, do it again and again and again" are the prevailing mottos. The seven deadly sins have become an accepted lifestyle.

Historian Will Durant has attributed the accumulation of our environmental problems to "undisciplined pursuit of individual pleasure." Few can argue with this evaluation. Unrestrained spending and abuse of credit, on both the national and individual levels, have led us to the edge of financial chaos. Years of wasting natural resources have led to panic, and even violence, in the face of enforced conservation. Undisciplined actions have produced undisciplined reactions.

Nor has the church escaped the blight of undisciplined living: there is ease today in Zion. Habitual gormandizing has produced flabby saints. Influence of the mass media, especially TV, has resulted in wasted time, dulled thinking, and perverted values. Emotions, exploited and distorted, run the gamut unchecked.

Consult your daily newspaper for further evidence. On every hand—in individual lives, in families, in schools, in society at large—the foundations of restraint are crumbling. And "when the foundations are being destroyed," the psalmist asked, "what can the righteous do?"

What *can* the righteous do in the midst of an undisciplined age? First, we must set our own house in order. As inhabitants of the modern wasteland, as poet T. S. Eliot characterized modern society, we can find hope only by first hearing and heeding the three words of the thunder: "Be charitable"; "Be compassionate"; "Be self-controlled." The final word here is also the final fruit of the Spirit (Gal. 5:23). In the Hindu *Upanishads,* source of Eliot's fable, self-control is the first of the three words. In a real sense, self-control is the first *and* the last, for the absence of this crowning grace negates the effect of the other graces.

THE NEGLECTED GRACE (FRUIT)

We have heard and read much in recent years about the gifts of the Spirit, but without the spiritual grace of self-discipline, the gifts will be ineffective, misused, or unused. We have heard and read perhaps somewhat less frequently about the fruit of the Spirit, particularly the first eight—love, joy, peace, long-suffering, gentleness, goodness, faith, meekness—but all too little about the final fruit, self-control or self-discipline. Most of us have heard sermons or series of sermons on the fruit of the Spirit in which the minister runs out of time or for some other reason gives short shrift to the final fruit, thus unwittingly illustrating the need to cultivate this neglected grace.

Rather than manifesting the spiritual grace of self-discipline and instilling it in our children, all too many of us are part of the current problem itself. The body of Christ seems to be afflicted with a form of St. Vitus dance, its members engaging in uncoordinated, uncontrolled, spasmodic twitching. Look at the weekly activities listed in the bulletin of the average evangelical church: meetings every night, a weekend seminar, a special workshop. We are busy-busy-busy believers. Are we so busy in the Lord's work that we get little or nothing *done* for the Lord? Have we equated busy-ness with effective service? There's so much movement but little momentum, so much activity but little action, so many programs but little progress. A frustrated believer recently summed it up: "I seem to be busy all the time, but I don't seem to be doing anything! I seem to be accomplishing nothing and getting nowhere!"

We ought to be busy in the Lord's work, but our activity must be self-disciplined to be effective. There's nothing wrong with Christ-honoring activities if they do not disrupt our priorities. The Lord never promised to reward us on the basis of busy-ness or time spent, but rather on the basis of faithful quality. Perhaps the laborers in Matthew 20 who went to work at 3:00 and 5:00 P.M. accomplished as much, as well, through their disciplined efforts as those who began work at 6:00 and 9:00 A.M.

BECOMING SELF-DISCIPLINED ENOUGH TO WRITE A BOOK ON SELF-DISCIPLINE

This book seeks to present the scriptural meaning and means of spiritual self-discipline. The inspiration for the book came during a sabbatical leave from my teaching duties at Arizona State University. I was involved in various research and writing projects, but somehow I just didn't seem to be able to "get it all together." I felt the need for greater self-discipline so I could "redeem the time."

One day as I sat in the reading room of the Houghton Library at

Harvard University, I noticed on one wall a portrait of William Ames, the great Puritan clergyman, and on the opposite wall a portrait of Thomas Wolfe, the American novelist. Ames seemed to represent the epitome of self-discipline, perhaps overly and rigidly so, whereas Wolfe has long had a reputation for lack of discipline, both in his life and in his writing.

"There must be a positive middle ground somewhere between the two extremes," I thought, "a genuine, spiritual self-discipline." But when I looked for literature on the subject, I found virtually nothing. I decided to study the Scriptures to look for the meaning and the means of true spiritual self-discipline. The more I studied, the more I realized how undisciplined I really was. I'm a long way from perfect yet, but I've improved with God's help.

This book is the result of that study. I trust that it will be used of God to help you learn the blessings and the benefits of genuine self-discipline. For only when the self is Spirit-controlled—for as we shall see, genuine self-control is Spirit-control—can we effectively use our spiritual gifts and be used by Him. Why not let Him make the necessary adjustments for a miracle recovery of control?

DEFINITION OF SELF-DISCIPLINE

1 / Self-Discipline:
What It Isn't

Self-discipline. Self-control. Self-restraint. Temperance. The words have strong negative connotations for most of us. (I can remember the deadly dullness of "Temperance Sundays" featured in the Sunday school quarterlies of my childhood.) They suggest the unpleasant prospect of being legalistically super-pious, an exacting killjoy, or even a "puritanical masochist."

In *The Screwtape Letters,* C. S. Lewis has master-devil Screwtape observe that the negative devaluation of such words as *puritan* and *discipline* has been one of "the really solid triumphs of the last hundred years," for it annually turns "thousands of humans from temperance, chastity, and sobriety of life." Satan delights in convincing us that to be self-disciplined is to be a spoilsport, a crapehanger, a wet blanket, a sourpuss. He must have clapped his hands over H. L. Mencken's famous definition of a Puritan as "someone who has the haunting fear that someone, somewhere may be having fun."

The unpopularity of the concept of self-discipline has rendered the word negative, and the negative associations of the word have, in turn, contributed to the unpopularity of the concept. It is necessary, therefore, to get beyond this vicious circle, beyond the stereotypes, beyond the general misconceptions of self-discipline. People either make too little of it or too much of it. Both extremes are dangerous.

SELF-DISCIPLINE IS NOT GODLINESS

There are some who would say that lack of discipline is sin, but this is not necessarily true. It is most assuredly, however, one of the "weights" spoken of in Hebrews 12:1—"Let us lay aside every weight, and the sin which doth so easily beset us, and let us run with patience the race that is set before us" (KJV). Lack of self-discipline is a hindrance in running an effective race for Christ. Often the line between the weight and the sin which so easily besets us is fine, indeed. If we know we should be more organized, controlled, and restrained—and who does not?—and if this hinders us from being and doing what God wants—and how could it not?—then after a certain point the lack of self-discipline does become sin. Such is the principle of James 4:17—"To him that knoweth to do good, and doeth it not, to him it is sin" (KJV). For example, I felt convicted to witness to an unsaved uncle about Christ, but I was too "busy," so I procrastinated by saying, "Well, one of these days, I'll go see him." Then I received word that my uncle had died of cancer. My lack of self-discipline had become sin!

In other cases, lack of discipline may lead to sin. Inconsistency in hiding God's Word in our hearts may cause us to err (Matt. 22:29) and even to fall (Ps. 119:11). In still other cases, lack of self-discipline may in itself constitute sin. First Samuel 12:23 says that failure to pray consistently is sin. Perhaps our lack of self-discipline is sin more often than we wish to admit, grieving and quenching the Spirit of God more often than we care to acknowledge.

If lack of discipline is not necessarily sin, discipline itself is not godliness. Although related, the two are not synonymous. Perhaps no group in history was more strictly "disciplined" than the Pharisees, "the separated ones." They meticulously pledged themselves to obey all traditions to the minutest degree and were absolute sticklers for ceremonial purity. Besides the required temple tax, they vowed to pay tithes of everything they possessed. Yet they were not godly (at least not those who were part of the degenerated Pharisaism of Jesus' day). In fact, Christ warned that the "righteousness" of the Pharisees was insufficient to gain entrance into the kingdom (Matt. 5:20). Just as they possessed a worthless self-righteousness, so they possessed a vain self-discipline or pseudo-discipline which prompted Christ's stern condemnation of their hypocrisy, false motivation, and lovelessness (Matt. 23). A member of their sect, Saul, exhibited considerable "discipline" in zealously persecuting the church, but he became godly only when he submitted to the risen Christ and was filled with the Spirit (Acts 9:17).

This Saul-transformed-to-Paul later admonished young Timothy: "Discipline yourself for the purpose of godliness" (1 Tim. 4:7 NASB). This Greek word translated "exercise" or "discipline" is *gumnazo* (source of our word *gymnasium*), which pictures Greek athletes engaging in strenuous exercise. The exercise Paul refers to is not physical, but is exercise of the mind, the emotions, the will, the spiritual part of a person. Paul suggests that, just as the Greek athlete disciplined himself for the purpose of winning physical contests, Timothy should discipline himself for the purpose of excelling in godly living.

SELF-DISCIPLINE IS NOT AN END IN ITSELF

Another scriptural principle thus becomes clear: self-discipline is not an end in itself, but a means to an end. The Greek athlete, after devoting months and years to strenuous training and agonizing struggle in the public games, would not have cast aside the victor's garland to glory in his regimen. Neither does the truly self-disciplined believer glory in spiritual calisthenics, but rather in their purpose—godly living.

Now we might logically ask, if discipline is not itself godliness, is it the *means* to godliness? The Scripture says emphatically no (Col. 2:23). If discipline led to godliness, the most disciplined individual would be the holiest—and holiness would be a result of human works. The most exacting disciplinary regimen conceivable is powerless to make a saint of a sinner. It can only make a very regimented sinner!

Perhaps the most disciplined sinner of all time was Benjamin Franklin. As a young man he began "the bold and arduous project of arriving at moral perfection." Admirable though the project was, Franklin did not achieve holiness. He later wrote in reference to the English evangelist George Whitefield: "He used sometimes to pray for my conversion, but never had the satisfaction of believing that his prayers were heard."

When Paul exhorted Timothy to exercise or discipline himself "for the purpose of godliness," he was simply reiterating the admonition he had given the Philippian believers: "Work out your salvation with fear and trembling" (Phil. 2:12). That is, work out what God has already worked in; discipline yourself so the godliness appropriated by faith can flourish.

SELF-DISCIPLINE IS NOT MERE ASCETICISM

The belief that self-discipline is a means to holiness is a form of asceticism, which teaches that rigorous self-denial, abstinence, austerity, and even self-inflicted pain are the means to a higher spiritual state. Paul condemns ascetic practices, both in the passage to Timothy discussed above and in his warning to the Colossians about Gnosticism: "Such practices pass for wisdom, with their self-imposed devotions, their self-humiliation, and their ascetic discipline [GOODSPEED], and unsparing severity of the body, but are of no value in combating fleshly indulgence" (MLB Col. 2:23). Whereas the ascetic, of whatever variety, trusts in external forms and practices to bring about internal spirituality, the truly self-disciplined believer trusts the indwelling Spirit of God to effect external practices that will permit spiritual graces to flourish.

Self-discipline is sometimes confused with two other austere Greek concepts, Spartanism and stoicism.

The Spartans, a warlike people who inhabited Sparta, a city in southern Greece, five hundred years before Christ, became a byword for severe discipline. At age seven boys were taken from their parents and enrolled in drill companies of fifteen, their military careers lasting until age sixty. Life was just one continuous trial of endurance, one extended push-up, with the gentler emotions suppressed. Such exacting training perhaps paid off for the Spartans in their victory over the Athenians in the Peloponnesian War. But toughness and severity alone do not necessarily constitute true self-discipline.

A form of Spartanism is reflected in the attitude of the believer who "religiously" jogs twenty miles a day because it "toughens the body, clears the mind, purges the emotions, and sanctifies the soul"—but who can't walk across the street to help a neighbor in need.

Stoicism was a Greek philosophy founded by Zeno in Athens around 300 B.C. Stoicism advocated calm, resigned acceptance of whatever transpired, with stern suppression of all emotions. There were Stoics at Mars Hill when Paul delivered his discourse there (Acts 17:18).

Some Christians have adopted what appears to be a neo-Stoic philosophy, which says, in effect, "Because I can accept whatever comes—pain, persecution, illness, poverty, even death—as God's highest good for me, I will be unmoved by any emotion, whether sadness or happiness, disappointment or elation, anger or gratification, fear or hope." But true Christian self-discipline is neither humanly self-sufficient nor disparaging of God-given emotions. Rather, through the Spirit's control, it achieves a balance of emotion, intellect, and will.

SELF-DISCIPLINE IS NOT IMMODERATION

This matter of balance, of moderation, is central to self-discipline. "Let your moderation be known unto all men," Paul admonished (Phil. 4:5 KJV). Believers are to manifest the ability to avoid excesses, to stay within reasonable bounds. Accordingly, the self-disciplined individual will be serious but not somber, precise but not pretentious, steady but not stodgy. He or she will, in short, be upright but not uptight.

There is a point at which even a positive quality, if pushed too far, becomes a negative one. Self-disciplined persons recognize the boundary and keep within it. We've probably all known Christian brothers and sisters whose attempts at self-discipline have taken them over the boundary of moderation. They're so organized, you'd better not disrupt their schedule! They're not just precise—they're persnickety. Ironically, they've become undisciplined in their attempts to achieve self-discipline! Such immoderate attempts at moderation are like truths that have lost their temper. There is an old Chinese proverb that says, "Excess paints a snake—and then adds legs!" Let's not put legs on the snake.

SELF-DISCIPLINE IS NOT CONSTRICTION

Self-disciplined people will cultivate the positive quality but avoid the closely associated negative quality. For example, they will be constrained (held in close bounds by the love of Christ in accordance with 2 Corinthians 5:14) but not constricted (squeezed in, compressed, made smaller—which is what this worldly system attempts to do: "Don't let the world around you squeeze you into its own mould" Rom. 12:2 PHILLIPS). True spiritual self-discipline holds believers in bounds but never in bonds; its effect is to enlarge, expand, and liberate.

Similarly, self-disciplined believers will be straight (upright, honest, and sincere) but not square (old-fashioned to the point of being unaware of recent happenings and trends). They will be regulated but not necessarily adjusted—neither to this worldly system nor to the stereotyped notion of what a self-disciplined Christian should be. They will keep an open mind, but not open at both ends. They will be doctrinal (faithfully, systematically learning the doctrines of Scripture) but not doctrinaire (dogmatically and ungraciously attempting to apply abstract dogma with little or no regard to practical living).

SELF-DISCIPLINE IS NOT LEGALISM

Rigid conformity to the letter of the law, with little regard for the spirit of justice, typifies legalism, a dangerous pitfall for believers cultivating self-discipline. Never legalistic, spiritually self-disciplined individuals are forbearing in a dual sense: they refrain from certain thoughts and deeds, holding themselves in check, and they control themselves under provocation, reacting to others in a patiently restrained manner.

Perhaps for these reasons the *Upanishads* are correct in placing "discipline" before "compassion" and "charity." Before we can be truly compassionate and give of ourselves, our time, and our means, we must first set our house in order. When this is done—and not for self-glorification according to the letter of the law—then God can work through us to help others.

The spiritually self-disciplined know how to say no. They have will power and "won't" power. While their discipline does not consist of legalistically and slavishly following a list of "don'ts," they adhere to the scriptural commands to abstain—from sexual immorality (1 Thess. 4:3), from sinful desires (1 Peter 2:11), from every kind of evil (1 Thess. 5:22). While accentuating the positive, they recognize the legitimate scriptural stress on the negative: "Blessed is the man who does not walk in the counsel of the wicked, or stand in the way of sinners, or sit in the seat of mockers" (Ps. 1:1).

But self-discipline is also a matter of *doing.* The Christian life is not a great escape, a mere series of evasive actions. When an immature Christian gave this report on his Christian life, "I don't _____ and I don't _____ and I don't go _____ and I avoid _____. . . ," a wise old saint said, "All you tell me is what you *don't* do! What do you *do?*"

SELF-DISCIPLINE IS . . .

Self-discipline is a spiritual grace or virtue that needs human development. It is the crowning fruit of the Spirit, cultivated and nurtured by Spirit-filled believers. The self-control or self-discipline of Christ is reproduced in the child of God by the power of the indwelling Spirit.

Just seven words form a compact scriptural definition of spiritual self-discipline: *"For to me, to live is Christ"* (Phil. 1:21).

We are able to live the Christ-life when we are totally submitted to the Spirit. In a real sense, the key to self-discipline is found in Paul's admonition: "Do not get drunk on wine, which leads to debauchery. Instead, be filled with the Spirit" (Eph. 5:18). A drunken person is not in control of his or her faculties, but a Spirit-filled believer is in control, for God works through our faculties. Thus, genuine self-control is Spirit-control; genuine self-discipline is Spirit discipline, nurtured and developed by the believer.

2 / Self-Discipline Is a Piece of Fruit
—But No Lemon

"This self-discipline *sounds* good—and even *possible*—on Sunday. And I start out on Monday with good intentions. But by Wednesday I've broken most of my resolutions, and, man, am I frustrated! I guess I'll just never be a very disciplined person." John's candid comment in my adult Sunday school class is typical of the experience of many frustrated believers. What's wrong?

First, we must recognize that Christian self-discipline comes not through human resolutions but through the working of the Spirit in the believer's new nature. The self-disciplined believer is resolute (determined, possessing a firm purpose), but not by fleshly resolve.

SELF-DISCIPLINE IS NEVER EASY

Self-discipline is never easy because it cuts against the grain of human nature. Paul graphically describes the frustration each of us has felt: "I do not understand what I do. For what I want to do I do not do, but what I hate I do. . . . I have the desire to do what is good, but I cannot carry it out. For what I do is not the good I want to do; no, the evil I do not want to do—this I keep on doing" (Rom. 7:15, 18–19). Does this sound like your latest effort at disciplined living?

29

Paul reveals the secret in the next chapter: doing what comes naturally results in frustrated failure; victory comes from doing what comes supernaturally. Self-discipline is not 99 percent perspiration and 1 percent inspiration, nor even 65 percent resolution and 35 percent revolution, as someone has described it. God doesn't work on fixed percentages. Rather, self-discipline is a healthy branch producing wholesome fruit.

Jesus uses the fruit metaphor in John 15, and Paul develops it in Galatians 5. "The fruit of the Spirit is love, joy, peace, patience, kindness, goodness, faithfulness, gentleness and self-control" (vv. 22–23). This nine-fold fruit of the Spirit comes from the fullness of the Spirit in the new nature; bearing fruit is natural to the healthy branch. I don't hear my orange tree or my grapefruit tree or my apricot tree out there groaning and straining and grunting to produce an orange, a grapefruit, or an apricot. The fruit appears in profusion as part of the natural process if the branches receive sufficient nourishment and nurture. Similarly, the nine-fold fruit of the Spirit appears in profusion, a product of the believer's new nature, if nourishment and nurture are provided.

Paul's use of the singular—*fruit* rather than *fruits*—suggests that all must be present. Yet discussions of the fruit of the Spirit[1] generally give short shrift to the final fruit, especially in its indispensable relation to the other eight.

The fruit of the Spirit is perhaps most analogous to an orange made up of nine distinct but connected segments.

Remove any one segment and the fruit is not only incomplete, but soon destroyed, for the other sections dry out and shrivel up. Similarly, without self-control, love may become saccharine sentimentality or consuming, self-defeating ardor; joy may become a heady euphoria that keeps us on the mountaintop building shrines; peace may become complaisance; patience may become leniency; kindness may become blandness; goodness may become self-righteousness; faithfulness may become slavishness; and gentleness may become weakness.

[1] One of the better, contemporary, discussions is John W. Sanderson's *The Fruit of the Spirit* (Grand Rapids: Zondervan Publishing House, 1972).

THE FRUIT OF THE SPIRIT

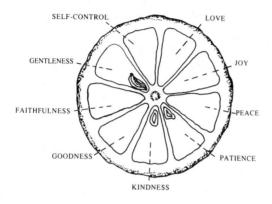

SELF-CONTROL IS BASIC

By the same token, without each of the other eight segments, true self-control cannot be developed or maintained. Each plays a distinct, essential part. For example, it is the love of Christ which *constrains* us (2 Cor. 5:14). The verb *synechō* conveys the idea of "exercising a controlling influence upon," "forcing into close bounds," "leaving us no choice," "compelling," "impelling," "urging," "overmastering," acting as "the very spring of our actions." Perhaps Kenneth Wuest has best captured the full import of the verse: "The love which Christ has [for me] presses on me from all sides, holding me to one end and prohibiting me from considering any other, wrapping itself around me in tenderness, giving me an impelling force." (*The New Testament: An Expanded* Translation). Christ's love for us (calling forth our love for Him) is the motivating force of self-discipline.

If self-discipline means "getting it all together," then joy, the second segment, is the means of "holding it all together." "The joy of the Lord is your strength" (Neh. 8:10). It was precisely for "the joy set before him" that Christ, the perfect model of self-discipline, "endured the cross, scorning its shame" (Heb. 12:2).

Peace, that tranquility and concord which only believers can know because they are in right relation to God and therefore to themselves and others, stands guard duty over our thoughts and emotions (Phil. 4:7). And Isaiah reminds us that God "will keep in perfect peace him whose mind is steadfast" on Him (26:3). Note the process: God's peace guards my mind, which, as I fix my thoughts on Him, produces peace, which, in turn, guards my mind, which produces peace. . . . This is not a vicious circle, but a virtuous one. God's inexplicable peace is both an influence upon and a result of self-discipline.

Perhaps patience, the fourth grace, is closest in meaning to self-discipline. The Greek word *makrothymia* is sometimes translated "forbearance," conveying the idea of patient endurance, of slowness in avenging injuries—essential characteristics of self-control. The Greek word appears twelve times in the New Testament—five times as an attribute of God, seven times as an attribute of the Spirit-filled believer. Paul makes it clear that this evenness in character and conduct is a divine quality, achieved not through fleshly resolve but through His grace. "So mighty is his majesty, he will nerve [empower, invigorate] you perfectly with strength for the cheerful exercise of endurance and forbearance in every situation" (Col. 1:1 GOODSPEED).

The next two segments of the fruit are in a sense like two sides of the same one: the word translated "kindness" conveys the idea of kind thoughts, the word translated "goodness" the idea of kind actions. The first is perhaps more accurately rendered "kindness," "usefulness," "beneficence," something very practical. Paul uses the second term in Ephesians 5, where, significantly, he is discussing the filling of the Spirit and its results: "For the fruit of the light consists in all goodness, righteousness and truth" (v. 9). And elsewhere he writes that our ability to admonish and edify other believers is dependent upon our being filled with this same attribute of goodness (Rom. 15:14).

The relationship between the seventh and ninth graces becomes clear when we realize that the word translated "faith" denotes "good faith"—that is, trustworthiness, honesty, integrity, sincerity—as well as "steadfastness" (stand-fast-ness) and "faithfulness." Perhaps the popular expression, "Keep the faith," captures something of the idea. And keep the faith is exactly what Paul did (2 Tim. 4:7); he was trustworthy and faithful to the end. It was precisely this quality of good faith that Jesus said the legalistic Pharisees did *not* keep (Matt. 23:23), and perhaps this is what Jesus meant when He asked, "When the Son of Man comes, will he find faith on the earth?" (Luke 18:8).

It is faithfulness that enables us to stand (2 Cor. 1:24), to be "grounded and settled" (Col. 1:23 KJV), "rooted," "built up," and "strengthened" in the faith (Col. 2:7). It is the much-needed ability to keep on serving with dependability and consistency; worshiping, working, witnessing, and watching; not growing weary in well-doing (2 Tim. 4:2; Gal. 6:9; 2 Thess. 3:13). It is godliness in the grind, righteousness in the routine. And anyone who thinks that this can be accomplished without lots of spiritual self-discipline hasn't tried it!

Perhaps the most misunderstood segment is "gentleness" or "meekness," so often equated with weakness. As someone has said, "If you think being meek is weak, try being meek for a week!" This Greek word can also be rendered "forbearance." The gentle person is, in the current idiom, "easygoing." In discussing the disciplined qualities of the Spirit-filled life, Paul stresses patience with people through gentleness: "Live a life worthy of the calling you have received. Be completely humble and gentle; be patient, bearing with one another in love" (Eph. 4:1–2; cf. Col. 3:12–13). Again, the quality is both a cause and an effect of self-discipline: we cannot be truly self-disciplined until we learn something about gentleness, and we cannot be genuinely gentle until we learn something of self-discipline.

The Greek word translated "self-control" appears, in several forms, six times in the New Testament. For example, the athlete striving for the prize practices rigorous self-control in all things (1 Cor. 9:25). Paul specifies self-control as one of the qualifications of an elder (Titus 1:8). And Peter lists it among eight great Christian virtues which are essential for fruit-bearing (2 Peter

1:5–8). "If these things be in you, and abound, they make you that ye shall neither be barren nor unfruitful in the knowledge of our Lord Jesus Christ" (v. 8 KJV).

SELF-CONTROL PRODUCES MORE FRUIT

Just as an orange carries within it seeds for producing more fruit, so the fruit of the Spirit, if nurtured, produces more fruit. One of the God-ordained purposes of fruit is the eventual production of more fruit. Accordingly, self-control is never self-serving and sterile. It is fertile and procreant, contributing both to new manifestations of the fruit of the Spirit and to the reproduction of fruit in the form of transformed lives.

The first appearance of *self-control (egkrateia)* in the New Testament is in Acts 24, where we read that Paul reasoned with Felix "on righteousness, self-control, and the judgment to come" (v. 25). It is little wonder that on this occasion Paul reasoned about "sobriety," "continence," "mastery of self," "mastery of the passions," as *egkrateia* is variously rendered. Felix, according to the Roman historian Tacitus, "revelled in cruelty and lust, and wielded the power of a king with the mind of a slave." Felix began his eight-year tenure as Roman procurator of Judea by seducing and marrying Drusilla, who was the wife of the king of a small Syrian state.

Paul's discourse on the need for mastery of the self met with a response all too common today: Felix was convinced of his need, even to the point of trembling, but he put it off until "I find it convenient" (Acts 24:25). Sound familiar?

Many believers, even well-meaning ones, say, "Sure, I know I need to be self-disciplined. I can't control my temper. My thoughts are often in the gutter. I overindulge. My life's a disorganized mess. Maybe next week I'll get organized. I'll get it all together—sometime." There is no record that Felix's "convenient time" ever came. Ours won't either. It's *never* convenient to be self-disciplined—only crucial.

3 / Self-Discipline Is
A Well-Mannered Puppy

My two sons had long been convinced that happiness is a warm puppy. So at our family council the vote on the question of getting a new puppy was three to one, my wife voting nay. (I wonder why.)

The six-week-old German shepherd was cute, cuddly, playful —and ill-mannered. She whined at night, polluted the family-room floor, and chewed everything in sight. After several trying months, she is finally learning to be quiet most of the time, to scratch on the door when nature calls, and to chew only on designated items.

Our puppy's "discipline" has been imposed externally through positive and negative reinforcement, a process that has demanded great self-discipline from the entire family (and some discipline imposed externally by parent on child). But if we want an obedient dog and a happy home, we must exert control!

The psalmist suggests that the self-disciplined person is like a successful dog trainer, who enforces good habits and curbs bad ones through the use of a muzzle. "Let me keep my mouth as with a muzzle, while the evil-doer is around," he writes (Ps. 39:1 MLB).

SELF-DISCIPLINE IS LIKE A BIT AND BRIDLE

What the muzzle is to the dog, the bit and bridle are to the horse. The horse, like the dog, must have discipline imposed externally. "We put bits into the mouths of horses," James says, "to make them obey us" (3:3).

The self-disciplined believer is analogous to a skilled equestrian bridling a spirited horse, knowing just when to rein in and when to release the reins. The bit and bridle harness the animal's fine energies, directing them to useful ends; without this restraint its movement is wasted and its energies dissipated. So it is with self-discipline in the Christian.

SELF-DISCIPLINE IS LIKE A SHIP'S RUDDER

The self-disciplined believer is also like an experienced pilot of a ship. James describes how great ships driven and tossed by fierce winds are steered by a rudder and are brought under control by the pilot (James 3:4). Perhaps it is significant that a recurring image used to depict the condition of modern society is that of a ship, listing hopelessly out of control and sinking. Norbert Wiener (who coined the term *cybernetics* from the Greek word meaning "helmsman") wrote in *The Human Use of Human Beings* that "in a very real sense we are shipwrecked passengers on a doomed planet." Similarly, in his novel *V,* Thomas Pynchon describes the symbolic scene of a helmsman painting the side of his sinking ship. Perhaps modern society, its entropy rapidly increasing, *is* a sinking ship.

Believers are empowered to steer their individual crafts with order and precision. This rudder is God's infallible Word and the guidance of the Holy Spirit.

SELF-DISCIPLINE IS LIKE FIRE OR
WATER UNDER CONTROL

Another metaphor used by James, this one to characterize the lack of self-discipline, is fire raging out of control. "Consider what a great forest is set on fire by a small spark," he writes (3:6). Fire under control is of benefit to humanity, but out of control it is most destructive. Fire warms and lights, but it also burns. It is estimated that fires kill over six thousand persons and destroy more than one billion dollars' worth of property every year in the U.S. Perhaps the crime of Prometheus, the mythological Titan who stole fire from heaven and gave it to man, was not so much in giving fire to man as it was in failing to teach him how to control it!

God—who is Himself "a consuming fire" (Heb. 12:29), whose Spirit is often symbolized by fire (Acts 2:3), whose word is like a fire (Jer. 23:29), who makes His servants "a flaming fire" (Ps. 104:4)—has given us spiritual fire, and He wants us to use it in a responsible, controlled way. But how like James and John we are in our lack of control and restraint! When the inhabitants of a Samaritan village did not welcome Jesus, these "Sons of Thunder" wanted to command fire to come down from heaven and consume them (Luke 9:54). But Jesus sternly rebuked them for their wrong spirit. (I once heard an evangelist vent his frustration at an unsaved man who did not respond to the gospel invitation: "All right then, *go* to hell and fry like a sausage!") We, no less than the disciples, need to learn the restrained use of God's fire.

Paul supplies one such lesson in Romans 12, where he gives a series of practical admonitions, none of which can be carried out without self-discipline. We are exhorted to leave vengeance to God (v. 19). By feeding our enemies when they are hungry and giving them drink when they are thirsty, we will "heap coals of fire" on their heads (v. 20). Note that they are only *coals,* not blazing flames. (Better the little coals that warm than the raging fire that consumes.) Remember, when you play with fire, you are apt to get burned (cf. Gal. 5:13–15).

Paul also warns of another kind of uncontrolled fire: the fire of enthusiasm. This takes the form of a zeal for God that is not based on knowledge (Rom. 10:2). Or, as Goodspeed renders it, they have a "sincere devotion . . . but it is not an intelligent devotion." Our enthusiasm for the things of the Lord must be tempered by knowledge (especially of His Word), by common sense (which is all too uncommon), and by tact. Some believers are "on fire for God" one week and "miss-firing" the next week. They "come under fire," and they cool off—maybe even freeze over. Then they hear a speaker or attend a seminar and get "all fired up" again—for two or three days.

SELF-DISCIPLINE IS LIKE A DYNAMO

Recently in a talk at a men's fellowship group, I was discussing the Greek word *dýnamis* in Acts 1:8, noting that it is the source of our word *dynamite* and emphasizing that we should have that kind of power in our lives. Afterward a local pastor came up and said, "Doesn't *dýnamis* more validly suggest 'dynamo,' also derived from the Greek? We don't need Christians who blow up with a big bang and then disappear; we need dynamos who consistently produce energy." He was right. The self-disciplined Christian is like an electrical generator functioning smoothly day in and day out, not creating energy, but transforming and channeling it into useful service.

A source of energy transformed by electrical generators is water, which, like fire, is beneficial when it is controlled and channeled, but destructive when it is out of control. The self-disciplined believer resembles the Colorado River controlled by the Hoover, Parker, and Davis Dams which produce domestic and irrigation water as well as electric power for Arizona and a large part of the Southwest. Without these great barriers to control the billions and billions of gallons of water, widespread destruction and death would result.

SELF-DISCIPLINE IS LIKE A
WELL-FORTIFIED CITY

Another scriptural illustration of the self-disciplined believer is found in references to a well-fortified city—its walls and its soldiers. Solomon alludes to such a city twice but from opposite perspectives. In one he shows the negative results of a lack of discipline: "Like a city whose walls are broken down is a man who lacks self-control" (Prov. 25:28). In the other he shows the positive value of self-discipline: "He who is slow to anger is better than the mighty, and he who rules his spirit, than he who captures a city" (16:32 MLB). In the first, the self-disciplined person is, by implication, a city protected by strong walls. In the second, the self-disciplined person is superior even to the mighty general who besieges a city and conquers it.

This comparison was especially meaningful in Solomon's day when every city was fortified by a thick brick or stone wall. Cities were usually built on hills with fortifications that followed the natural contour of the land. Throughout the Old Testament, these fortifications symbolize strength, security, and salvation (e.g., Zech. 2:4–5; Isa. 26:1). God promised to make Jeremiah "a fortified wall of bronze" against which the ungodly could not prevail (Jer. 15:20). *Without* self-discipline we are defenseless, exposed to attack and easy prey for the enemy. We are rather like the young man who was commissioned to guard the village entrance and close the massive wood and iron gates whenever hostile forces approached. One day he dawdled at his post and didn't hear the sentry's warning. Enemy soldiers rode freely into the village and slaughtered its inhabitants.

SELF-DISCIPLINE IS LIKE MILITARY TRAINING

The self-disciplined believer is likened not only to the conquering general but also to the enlisted recruit, who has given up all civilian enterprises so he can please his commanding officer. Paul, in urging Timothy to be faithful in teaching others, also uses a military image: "Take your part with others in enduring hardships as a good soldier of Jesus Christ. No one when engaged in military service allows himself to become involved in civilian pursuits, in order that he may please the one who enlisted him as a soldier" (2 Tim. 2:3–4 WUEST, Ex. Trans.). Just as the Roman legionnaires subjected themselves to discipline in the service of the emperor, so Christians are to be disciplined in the service of the King of Kings.

A good soldier *abstains* and *sustains,* each being a part of self-discipline. He renounces everything that will displease his commander. (Note the recurrence of such words as *shun, depart from, purge from, flee,* and *avoid* in 2 Timothy 2:14–26.) He renounces not only the evil but also the less-good. He doesn't get entangled in *pragmateiais*—affairs, businesses, occupations, transactions of civilian life. These are not illegitimate or even questionable activities. They are simply activities, perhaps "good" in themselves, that often become enemies of the "better" and the "best."

A familiar example of legitimate activity taking precious time from the "better" and the "best" is TV watching. According to a recent estimate, the average eighteen-year-old has watched, in his or her lifetime, 15,000 hours of television. Even perfect attendance in Sunday school during that time would only add up to approximately 900 hours! What does this contrast say about our priorities?

The good soldier also sustains. He endures, bears up under, or withstands. And the well-disciplined Christian soldier also prevails. He or she doesn't just passively bear, always on the defensive, but forbears and actively, aggressively triumphs.

SELF-DISCIPLINE IS LIKE ATHLETIC TRAINING

Paul repeatedly uses another metaphor to characterize the self-disciplined believer—the well-trained Greek athlete. "If anyone competes as an athlete, he does not receive the victor's crown unless he competes according to the rules" (2 Tim. 2:5). The verb translated "strive for masteries" in the King James Version is *athleo,* source of our word *athlete.* In order to be eligible for the victor's crown—a wreath woven of laurel, ivy, and oak leaves—the athlete was required to discipline himself according to the regulations, both in preparation for and participation in the contest. He was required to spend ten months in rigorous training, which included prescribed exercises, restricted activities, subjection to extremes of weather, and a self-denying diet that prohibited wine and rich foods. In the contest itself he was required to observe strict conditions, such as staying within the designated bounds of the course (no shortcuts permitted!) and wearing lightweight clothing. If he were to break any of these training rules or contest regulations, he would be disqualified.

The point is sobering indeed. If a believer lacks the self-discipline to follow the training rules and the rules of the game, God may even pull him out and let him "warm the bench" while others run the race!

With an even greater sense of urgency, Paul uses the same figure of speech in 1 Corinthians 9:24–26. He tells them to "make tracks for the finish line!"

Paul changes from the image of a runner to that of a boxer. "I am like a boxer, who does not waste his punches. I harden my body with blows and bring it under complete control, to keep from being rejected myself after having called others to the contest" (1 Cor. 9:26–27 GNB). The picture is that of perfect control—no wasted effort, every movement contributing to the motivating purpose. The physical is in balanced subjection (not put *down,* but put *under*) to the mental and spiritual. Perhaps this passage gives the clearest sanction for the self-discipline of a Christian: just as the athlete received a victor's garland for observing the rules of discipline and a penalty for not doing so, the Christian receives an eternal reward for his disciplined service and disapproval for his undisciplined wasting of his talents.

SELF-DISCIPLINE IS LIKE A YOKE

At least one other image, this one a composite figure used by Jesus, appears in Scripture to characterize the self-disciplined believer. In tenderly inviting those who are weary and overburdened to come to Him for rest, Jesus said: "Bend your necks to my yoke, and learn from me, for I am gentle and humble-hearted; and your souls will find relief. For my yoke is good to bear, my load is light" (Matt. 11:29–30 NEB). The yoke—a wooden bar or frame fitted around the necks of two draft animals for harnessing them together—was a Jewish metaphor for both discipline and discipleship.

The yoke denoted subjection to authority and submission to command. Just as the ox bent the neck to the yoke, so the believer should patiently submit as a disciple to the authority and instruction of Christ. To accept this discipline is to become a disciple, and being a disciple requires yet more discipline. The disciple, in denying himself and taking up his cross daily (Luke 9:23–26) to follow Christ is identifiable with Christ and the cross.

The yoke figure teaches several important lessons about self-discipline. Just as the yoke denotes both hardship and help (if a beast must pull, the yoke actually aids him), so self-discipline suggests the two: it is arduous, but without it there is no true discipleship and consequently no fruit with its accompanying blessing and reward. Further, the passage suggests that there are two forms of yokes: one that galls and wearies us, and the one Jesus gives, which paradoxically rests and refreshes us. So it is with self-discipline: there is a false discipline that exhausts and enslaves, and there is genuine spiritual self-discipline that renews and liberates.

Wanting to make the concept clear to us, the Holy Spirit used a variety of images. Whether it's a trainer with muzzled dog, an equestrian with bridled horse, a helmsman with responsive ship, fire or water under control and therefore beneficial, a dynamo producing energy, a city protected by strong fortifications, a general conquering a city, a recruit abstaining and sustaining in order to please his commanding officer, an athlete striving to win the prize, or a draft animal/servant/disciple submitting to the hardship/help of the yoke—they all illustrate *self-discipline*.

DOCTRINE AND SELF-DISCIPLINE

4 / A Little Bit Here and a Little Bit There: The Doctrinal Basis of Self-Discipline

"Tell me what you believe or don't believe," someone has said, "and I'll tell you what you're likely to do or not do." Practice reflects belief, and right practice must be grounded in right belief. The oldest meaning of discipline is "a branch of knowledge or learning" or "a field of study." Genuine self-discipline must be based upon the doctrines of Scripture, and the doctrines of Scripture can be learned only through spiritual self-discipline.

THE DISCIPLINE OF LEARNING DOCTRINE

The prophet Isaiah's clear, repeated warnings of imminent judgment at the hands of the Assyrians were met with debased mockery by the drunkards of Ephraim. "To whom is he explaining his message?" (28:9) they asked. "Who does Isaiah think *he* is to presume to teach us?" "Whom shall he make to understand doctrine?" "Does he take us to be little babies just weaned?" Then the scoffers mocked Isaiah's speaking with a song of rhyming monosyllables imitating the babblings of a child: *"Sav lasav, sav lasav; Kav lakav, kav lakav; Z'er sham, z'er sham,"* which could be interpreted as: "Law on law, law on law; saw on saw, saw on saw; a little bittie here and a little bittie there." (Today it would no doubt be sung to a tune such as "Old Mac-

Donald Had a Farm.'') But in verse 13, the Lord responds to their blasphemous mockery by imitating the sing-song and representing it as the unknown language of the conqueror.

The passage offers several important principles. First, those who most lack self-discipline, such as these drunken Ephraimites, most scorn the simplicity, the repetition, the routine required to learn both doctrine and discipline.

Second, these scoffers unwittingly expressed the only way doctrine *can* be learned: "Order on order, line on line, a little here, a little there" (Isa. 28:10 NASB). The great truths and principles of Scripture cannot be learned overnight; it takes years and years of regular, consistent, disciplined study—a little at a time. Accordingly, Paul admonished Timothy to "study" in order to show himself "approved unto God" (2 Tim. 2:15 KJV). The word translated "study" *(spoodazo)* suggests not only the spectator's shout of encouragement to the Olympic runner ("May you win the race"), but also the encouragement of a Greek mother to her son as he leaves for school ("May you do your best"), and the words of a dying father to his eldest son ("Take good care of all these things"). Such tasks require a great deal of patient determination.

Early in his ministry, Martin Luther had to learn this lesson of disciplined study of doctrine—the hard way. Rather than preparing a sermon, he went before his congregation hoping that God would give him the words to utter. Luther said later that God had spoken to him. He had said, "Martin, you're unprepared!"

There will be setbacks, discouragements, even seeming regression in our disciplined learning of doctrine. But as James reminds us, perseverance must be allowed to finish her work (1:4). Note how Peter brings together knowledge of doctrine, discipline, and patience when he urges us to add to our "knowledge, self-control, and to self-control, perseverance" (2 Peter 1:6).

A MAJOR CAUSE OF THE LACK OF SELF-DISCIPLINE

Doctrine, then, can be learned only through the patient self-disciplined study of the revealed Word of God. Solomon warned that "where there is no revelation [in the Old Testament times the prophetic ministry, in our time the completed canon of Scripture], the people cast off restraint; but blessed is he who keeps the law" (Prov. 29:18). The Hebrew verb "cast off restraint," which is translated "perish" in the King James Version, conveys the idea of "running wild" or "becoming unbridled." Failure to read and study the Word of God is tantamount to not having the Word of revelation at all.

It's not enough, of course, merely to read the Word; we must let it read us. We must submit to its discipline. For every Scripture is breathed by God, Paul says. Therefore, it is "profitable for doctrine [Paul uses this word nineteen times, fifteen in the Pastoral Epistles alone], for reproof [for conviction], for correction, for instruction in righteousness" (2 Tim. 3:16 KJV). "Instruction" here conveys the idea of correcting mistakes and curbing passions. The Word disciplines us in righteous, moral living.

The solid food of the Word of God, the writer of Hebrews says, is for mature believers, for those "who by constant use have trained themselves to distinguish good from evil" (Heb. 5:14). The Greek word here translated "trained" (or "exercised" in the King James Version) is a form of the word *gumnazo,* "to train in gymnastic discipline." This involves the constant, habitual practice of studying and the constant feedback of the discipline of the Word, the solid food. It is the Word of God that gives order to our steps (Ps. 119:133).

It was said that whenever Lord Cairns entered the British Parliament, his very presence brought peace, harmony, order. What was his secret? He said that it was his habit to spend no less than two hours each morning in disciplined meditation on the Scriptures and in prayer.

GOD IS THE SOURCE OF DISCIPLINE

Perfect discipline is to be found in God alone, the source of order, the epitome of self-control. Only He is unaffected by entropy, the natural tendency toward disorder and chaos. James tells us that every good and every perfect gift "cometh down from the Father of lights, with whom is no variableness, neither shadow of turning" (1:17 KJV). The word here translated "turning" *(tropes)* is the word from which we get *entropy.* In the spiritual realm only God escapes the effects of disorder.

In emptying Himself of His divine prerogatives and taking the form of a servant (Phil. 2), God the Son provided the perfect example of self-discipline. And God the Holy Spirit, who, in creating the world, moved upon the formless void, is Himself the great restrainer of undisciplined iniquity (2 Thess. 2:7). Further, the Holy Spirit empowers us, activating the gift of self-discipline which is the fruit of His infilling (Gal. 5).

SATAN: AUTHOR OF DISORDER

If God is "not the author of confusion but of peace" (1 Cor. 14:33 KJV), then His adversary—and ours—is the author and instigator of disorder. The word here translated "confusion" also means: commotion, unsettled state, tumult and sedition, the stirring up of discontent, resistance, and rebellion against authority. How aptly these phrases describe Satan's original and continuing activity. In Luke 21:9 the same word characterizes the wars and commotions of the end time. James uses the word in describing wisdom that is "earthly, unspiritual, of the devil" (3:15). Such a wisdom, he says, is accompanied by disharmony, disorder, anarchy—in contrast to the heavenly wisdom, which is "first of all pure, then peaceable, *forbearing*" (v. 17 MOFFATT).

Satan, through self-will and sedition, introduced disorder into God's orderly creation. Pandemonium, Milton's name for the capital of hell, has become an appropriate designation for any place or scene of wild confusion and noise. It is Satan's intent to make every heart, every home, every assembly a Pandemonium —without order, control, or restraint. It is God's intent to bring order, control, discipline. If "order is the first law of heaven," as Alexander Pope said, disorder is the first law of hell.

Note the logical deduction to be drawn at this point: If the spirit of Satan is the spirit of disorder, then the extent to which my life manifests disorder, unrestraint, and lack of control is an indication of the extent to which the spirit of Satan has influence over me. That's startling, but I believe it's a valid conclusion. Isn't it time we started manifesting the "first law of heaven"?

SELF-CONTROL: A MARK OF SPIRITUALITY

Paul told the Corinthian believers, who seemed to have more disorder than order, that genuine self-control is a mark of spirituality: "The spirits of prophets are subject to the control of prophets" (1 Cor. 14:32), or "The gift of speaking God's message should be under the speaker's control" (GNB). Without the *fruit* of the Spirit, the gifts of the Spirit will be misused or unused. True self-control, the Scriptures suggest, is really Spirit-control, whereas being controlled by the carnal self is essentially being in the sway of Satan, for the spirit of the fleshly self is the spirit of Satan. (Note the recurrence of the personal pronoun "I" in the account of Lucifer's fall in Isaiah 14:12–14.)

The basis of undisciplined living is also the basis of the sin problem: self. This is not to say, of course, that being undisciplined is necessarily sin, although it may be or it may lead to sin. Conversely, as we noted in chapter one, self-discipline is not sanctification, nor even the means by which it is achieved. We must confront the enemy and, like Pogo, recognize him for what he is—ourselves—and then allow the Spirit of God to subdue and control him. Our great need, and a starting place in the acquiring of self-discipline, is to surrender our soul to Christ, yielding the keys to Him for His control.

DIVINE GRACE: MEANS OF ORDER

Sin is missing the God-ordained mark, the perfect order. It is distorting God's intent into chaos or substituting illegitimate means to achieve God-ordained ends. God's means of bringing order out of sin's disorder, of transforming man's control by Satan to control by the Spirit is grace. The word for grace is *charis,* that which transforms an unpleasing, disordered circumstance into a pleasing, ordered one. Ephesians 2:1–10 depicts the unregenerate person as being unrestrained, manifestly out of control (in reality under Satan's control) until God's grace transforms him or her miraculously into a manifestly self-controlled (that is, under the Spirit's control), well-ordered masterpiece ("workmanship" is the Greek word *poiema,* source of our word *poem*) productive of good works. Appropriately, the nine segments of the fruit of the Spirit are sometimes called "graces."

Who comes to your mind when you think of a grace-full person, an individual so controlled by the Spirit of God that he or she continually manifests the nine graces of the Spirit? Two godly women come to my mind: my mother and my mother-in-law, both now with the Lord. Annie and Christine always seemed to be under control, even in the most trying circumstances. And wherever they went, their presence conveyed a calming effect on everyone. Talk about charisma! They had a divine grace that only God can bestow.

Too often we relegate grace to the initial experience of conversion, failing to recognize that it is by grace that we *grow* (2 Peter 3:18). The grace of God is essential for learning the discipline of renunciation. Paul wrote, "The grace of God that brings salvation has appeared to all men. It teaches us to say 'No' to ungodliness and worldly passions, and to live self-controlled, upright and godly lives in this present age" (Titus 2:11–12). Grace teaches us to live lives of order and self-mastery.

As we continue to walk in the Spirit, appropriating the grace of God and learning through the schooling of grace, we grow and mature. Christian maturity is the process of becoming self-controlled, which in its true sense is becoming God-controlled, because God's grace works through our faculties. Thus Paul could say, "I can do all things through Christ, which strengtheneth me" (Phil. 4:13 KJV).

THE RELATIONSHIP BETWEEN SELF-DISCIPLINE AND GROWTH

One of the few Christian writers who allude to the relationship between self-discipline and personal growth is Richard Halverson. In *Christian Maturity* he writes: "There is a discipline involved in Christian growth. The rapidity with which a man grows spiritually and the extent to which he grows, depends upon this discipline. It is the discipline of the means." Some believers mature more rapidly and more deeply than others because they make better use of God-given means of growth, such as Bible study, prayer, fellowship, and witnessing. Self-discipline is essential in each of these areas, and each serves to foster more self-discipline—yet another virtuous circle. For example, obedience to the command, "Pray continually" (1 Thess. 5:17), requires genuine self-discipline. And as one prays regularly, he or she is renewed and strengthened for greater self-discipline. The very nature of prayer itself provides order in the midst of chaos. Novelist Saul Bellow has noted this parallel between art and prayer: "Art has something to do with the achievement of stillness in the midst of chaos. A stillness which characterizes prayer, too, and the eye of the storm, . . . an arrest of attention in the midst of distraction." In this sense, your life and mine, when they are disciplined, are true works of art—what the poet Robert Frost called "a momentary stay against confusion."

If Halverson is correct in saying that Christian growth and maturity are dependent on "the discipline of the means," one of the means of self-discipline is the Christian doctrine of divine testing or chastening. The writer of the Book of Hebrews admonishes us not to "make light of the Lord's discipline," for God, the loving Father, "disciplines those whom He loves." Therefore, we are to "endure hardship as discipline" (12:5–7). The writer goes on to say, "Of course, no discipline seems at the time enjoyable but painful; later on, however, it affords those schooled in it the peaceable fruitage of an upright life" (12:11 MLB). The word translated "discipline" here is the Greek word *paideia* (training, instruction, chastisement, correction), source of our word *pedagogy* and the same word Paul uses in Titus 2:12 to describe the discipline of grace. Learning self-discipline through the Lord's externally imposed discipline produces "the fruit of peace which grows from upright character" (WILLIAMS).

Manifold trials—pain, suffering, adversity, affliction, hardship, misfortune, reversals—if encountered *in the Spirit,* will produce self-discipline. Accordingly, James urges us to consider such trials pure joy for "the trial and proving of your faith bring out endurance and steadfastness and patience" (1:3 AMPLIFIED)—the essence of self-discipline.

Have you ever heard anyone say, "Be careful about praying for patience. God might answer your prayer"? God teaches us patience through trials and adversity. Isn't it through pain and suffering that we learn and grow? Think of the most self-disciplined person you know. Very likely that person has undergone considerable adversity. Suffering can smooth out the rough edges of character.

Elmer Lappen illustrated this principle. He suffered greatly with rheumatoid arthritis and in his last years was confined to a wheelchair. Every day and every night brought almost unbearable pain, but even until death Elmer manifested a sweet, self-disciplined spirit as he faithfully bore witness for Christ on the university campus.

REWARD AND JUDGMENT

The sanctions and motives of self-discipline must also be firmly based on biblical teaching—the divine promise of reward for self-disciplined stewards, and the divine warning of loss for those who are undisciplined. Jesus' parable of the testing of servants graphically contrasts these two types of people (Matt. 24:36–51; Luke 12:41–48). The former is faithful and wise, providing food for the household until the goodman of the house returns with commendation and reward. Notice that the Lord commends and rewards not ability, but faithfulness. To remain faithful in a sinful age requires great self-discipline. Therefore, our rewards will be determined to a large degree by how self-disciplined we are.

Although he knew better, the unfaithful servant did not make proper preparations. The servant's lack of self-discipline is clearly manifest both in what he fails to do and in what he does.

He loses control and beats the servants under him; he yields to gluttony and drunkenness; and he wastes the substance, gifts, and time allotted to him. Upon his master's return he, like the five foolish virgins (Matt. 25), suffers great loss and retribution. Jesus was enjoining watchfulness, and what is watchfulness if it is not self-disciplined living? The stern warning is for us all: "Be on your guard, so that your hearts may not be loaded down with self-indulgence, drunkenness, and worldly worries, and that day, like a trap, catch you unawares" (Luke 21:34 WILLIAMS).

Each believer has a rendezvous at the judgment seat of Christ, where he or she will receive recompense for the deeds done in the body (2 Cor. 5:10). This, different from the Great White Throne Judgment of unbelievers (Rev. 20:11–15), is when believers' works will be judged and be the basis of rewards or the suffering of loss (1 Cor. 3:12–15). It is the *Bema* judgment, that tribunal where Greek athletes, victorious through self-discipline, would be crowned with garlands of glory. But for many believers it will be a solemn accounting for the results of self-indulgence and for talents unused and undeveloped.

If we will judge ourselves, we shall not be judged, Paul said (1 Cor. 11:31). If we discipline ourselves, we shall not have to be disciplined externally. Self-judgment avoids chastisement; self-discipline precludes divine discipline and produces works that shall withstand the fire of God's testing.

BIBLICAL EXAMPLES OF
SELF-DISCIPLINE

5 / Burning Bushes and Fiery Tongues: Self-Discipline In the Lives of Bible Figures

An ancient Chinese proverb says, "Not the cry, but the flight of the wild goose, leads the flock to fly and follow." Clear example gains more followers than abstract precepts. Perhaps this is what prompted one clergyman to observe, "People look at me six days in the week to see what I mean on the seventh."

The Word of God provides abundant, concrete examples of the blessings of self-discipline as well as the blight of self-indulgence. In the final chapter of his epistle, James presents two contrasting lifestyles: undisciplined self-indulgence at the expense of others versus patient, self-disciplined endurance in anticipation of the Lord's return. In the first six verses James addresses the selfish rich: "[Here] on earth you have abandoned yourselves to soft (prodigal) living and to [the pleasures of] self-indulgence and self-gratification. You have fattened your hearts in a day of slaughter" (v. 5 AMPLIFIED). Two graphic verbs describe the utter lack of self-discipline. The first, *truphao*, meaning "to live [revel] in soft [wanton] luxury," is derived from a root meaning "to break down." It depicts a life of unrestrained luxury that ends by destroying the strength of both body and soul.

The second verb, even stronger and more negative, is *spatalao,* "to plunge into dissipation," "to indulge self to the full," "to live in wanton riotousness." Such living, according to James, has the effect of fattening people like cattle for the slaughter—the inevitable judgment.

In verse six, James further accuses these people. They resent self-discipline because it reproves them, and they persecute those who practice such discipline. "Ye have condemned and killed the just" (KJV)—Jesus and all who follow His example.

Alcibiades, friend of Socrates, was often riotous and undisciplined. He used to say to the more disciplined philosopher, "Socrates, I hate you; for every time I see you, you show me what I am." Self-discipline is a silent reproach to self-indulgence, but if it is genuine and spiritual it does not flaunt itself, but patiently endures, as Jesus did when He offered no resistance in the face of death.

Paul, in describing the self-indulgent disobedience which resulted in the wilderness wandering of the Israelites for forty years, says: "Now these things occurred as examples, to keep us from setting our hearts on evil things as they did" (1 Cor. 10:6).

In contrast, James admonishes us (5:7), in the light of the imminent return of Christ, to practice self-discipline, taking as our example those who have spoken in the Lord's name and those who are called blessed because they endured and persevered. Let's take a look at the examples of Moses and the children of Israel.

MOSES HAD 3,000,000 DISCIPLINE PROBLEMS

Try to imagine approximately three million self-indulgent, intemperate, complaining men, women, and children leaving Egypt for the Promised Land. God performed miracle after miracle on their behalf—the ten plagues, the parting of the Red Sea and destruction of Pharaoh and his armies, the guidance of the pillar of cloud and fire, the sustenance of manna and water from the rock, the victory over their enemies—yet they repeatedly forgot His blessings and lapsed into stubborn disobedience, idolatry, and open rebellion. They never learned spiritual self-discipline, and consequently the original generation was condemned to wander and die in the wilderness, never reaching the Promised Land. Paul reiterates how they lost all restraint, abandoning themselves to idolatry and revelling. They "sat down to eat and drink, and rose up to play" (1 Cor. 10:7 KJV). Twenty-three thousand died in one day as punishment for their fornication (v. 8). Exodus 32 describes the death of three thousand in retribution for the idolatrous orgy around the golden calf.

In their stubborn self-indulgence, the Israelites are appropriately described as being stiffnecked or stiffhearted (Exod. 32:9; 33:3, 5; 34:9; Deut. 9:6, 13. The Greek equivalent, used by Stephen in his scathing address to the Sanhedrin (Acts 7:51), has as its stem *scleros,* from which is derived our word *sclerosis,* a hardening of bodily tissues. Continued self-indulgence hardens the heart, making one set in one's ways. Self-discipline should be developed when the heart is tender and when the neck is submissive to the yoke of authority. But it is never too late to learn self-discipline if the spirit is willing, for God promised to perform a heart-transplant, removing the stony heart and giving a tender heart of flesh (Ezek. 11:19).

The obstinate Israelites stand in sharp contrast to the generally consistent self-disciplined Moses. In his lyrical farewell address to the whole assembly of Israel, Moses solemnly warned them of the dangers of self-indulgence: "Jeshurun ["upright one"—poetic ideal name for Israel or else ironic] fattened and grew restive—ay, you fattened, gross and gorged—they forsook God who had made them, scorned the steadfast One, their succour" (Deut. 32:15 MOFFATT). (Moffatt used the highly connotative word *gross* fifty years before its current popularity!) Israel "grew bloated and sleek," the New English Bible puts it. "Gorge yourself, and you do become fat and corpulent," Goodspeed renders it. The language denotes excess, utter lack of self-restraint. "Restive" accurately characterizes their state, meaning not only restless, discontented, and unsettled, but also unruly, obstinately refusing to go forward, like a balky mule.

Note Moses' suggestion of a gradual, sequential movement

downward: Figuratively speaking, Israel overate, gorged itself, grew fat, bloated, and finally became *covered* with fat—*then* forsook God. Such is always the way with self-indulgence: it engenders more of itself until, in a vicious circle, it leads one to forsake God. Actions evolve into habits, habits into patterns, patterns into a lifestyle.

Someone has expressed it this way: "Sow an act, and you reap a habit; sow a habit, and you reap a character; sow a character, and you reap a destiny." Genuine self-discipline means breaking bad habits and forming good ones. Practicing good actions through self-discipline makes doing them easier, and when they are habitual we can take pleasure in them. When our actions please God and us, we do them frequently, and then, by frequency of act, they grow into good habits.

MOSES: OUR EXAMPLE

Among Old Testament figures, perhaps none exemplifies self-discipline more than Moses, the great lawgiver. (Moses has always won, hands down, in every poll I've taken to determine the most self-disciplined figure in the Old Testament.) It's only logical that anyone who successfully leads and disciplines a group of people must first master himself. The self-mastery of Moses did not come easily: he had at least three serious lapses.

The first forty years of his life were spent in the royal Egyptian court. There Moses was instructed in the arts and sciences of the Egyptians. He developed highly disciplined oratorical and leadership qualities. Stephen says he was "learned in all the wisdom of the Egyptians, and was mighty in words and deeds" (Acts 7:22 KJV). Yet Moses refused to be known as "the son of Pharaoh's daughter; Choosing rather to suffer affliction with the people of God, than to enjoy the pleasures of sin for a season" (Heb. 11:24–25 KJV). His decision illustrates several important characteristics of self-discipline. First, he had a sound, godly value system and set of priorities. "He considered the 'reproach of Christ' more precious than all the wealth of Egypt" (Heb. 11:26 PHILLIPS). He was not self-indulgent or materialistic. Further, he was able, as the self-disciplined person must be, to take the long view, not sacrificing the ultimate on the altar of the immediate. "He looked steadily at the ultimate, not the immediate, reward" (Heb. 11:26 PHILLIPS). Only spiritual self-discipline enables one to make decisions "with eternity's values in view."

Moses also showed emotional self-control: "He left Egypt, not fearing the king's anger; he persevered because he saw him who was invisible" (Heb. 11:27). Finally, he endured, persisted, and held his course unflinchingly, strengthened by his vision of the invisible God.

MOSES AND THE FRUIT OF THE SPIRIT

The more unrestrained and self-indulgent the Israelites became, the more self-disciplined Moses was required to be. Significantly, the man through whom God was to give the Law manifested the nine fruits of the Spirit specified in Galatians 5. What greater manifestation of *love* can one find than Moses' willingness to sacrifice his own life for his people after their apostasy with the golden calf? "If thou wilt forgive their sin—; and if not blot me, I pray thee, out of thy book which thou hast written" (Exod. 32:32 KJV). And what greater expression of *joy* can one find than Moses' song of the redeemed in Exodus 15? Moses' illustrious career also shows numerous examples of *peace* in its various forms: individual peace, peace with God, and communal peace (freedom from strife, variance, envy, jealousy). Perhaps the secret of this grace in Moses' life is most clearly indicated after the victory over the Amalekites when Moses built an altar and called it *Jehovah-Nissi,* "The Lord is my banner."

Moses also manifested *patient* endurance in obedience to God, despite pressure to deny Him. Again and again Moses endured complaints, criticism, threats, and open rebellion against his leadership, mediating between the sinful people and a Holy God. Even when his own sister and brother criticized him, he bore it with *gentleness.* Numbers 12:3 says that Moses was the most gentle, or meek, person on earth. Moses did not defend himself against the criticism, nor did he cry out to God for vengeance.

Rather he besought God to heal Miriam when she suffered for her sins with leprosy. Such a gentle attitude is always the result of humility. To be meek and gentle when all around you—even your brother and sister—are arrogant and insensitive requires the utmost in self-discipline.

It is clear that the *goodness* of Moses was a reflection of God's goodness. When Moses sought a renewed vision from God, He made all His goodness pass before Moses (Exod. 33:19; 34:6). And when Moses came down from Mount Sinai, his face shone with the glory of God. But Moses was unaware of it (Exod. 34:29). Similarly, true self-discipline and its effects are always more obvious to *others;* in fact, the moment we pride ourselves in our self-control and flaunt it, we have lost control!

Moses' faith and *faithfulness* are emphasized not only in Hebrews 11 but also in Hebrews 3, which, in turn, echoes Numbers 12:7 (kjv): "Moses . . . is faithful in all mine house." He was loyal, dependable, in carrying out his God-given duties.

MOSES WASN'T PERFECT

It would be satisfying to end the discussion of Moses on that positive note, but despite all his admirable qualities he was human like you and me. He had at least three major lapses in self-control, each having far-reaching effects. The first lapse came at the end of his forty years in Egypt. When he saw an Egyptian beating a Hebrew, he lost control and killed the Egyptian (Exod. 2:11–12). Zeal, even for the most righteous cause, is not enough; it must be tempered by knowledge (Rom. 10:2). Consequently, Moses did not have sufficient self-discipline to command respect from his people. The Hebrews rejected him as their leader, and God sent him to the back side of the Midian desert for a forty-year post-graduate course in self-discipline. During this period, Moses was a shepherd and he thereby learned the fundamentals of restraint and self-control, as well as firsthand knowledge of survival in the territory surrounding the Gulf of Aqaba, the area through which he would subsequently lead the Israelites.

Moses' second forty-year period was climaxed by his confrontation with the burning bush that was not consumed. This phenomenon, typifying Jehovah as a "consuming fire" (Deut. 4:24; 9:3; Heb. 12:29), provided for Moses a graphic symbol of self-discipline: the bush flamed but never burned *up* or *out;* the fire represented power under control—just what Moses needed to learn.

Moses' doubt concerning his leadership abilities (Exod. 4:1, 10) revealed that he had learned something about meekness in the forty years since he attempted to take the slavery situation into his own hands by killing the Egyptian. But his persistent objections, in spite of miraculous signs and God's promises to "be with his mouth," suggest that he may have over-reacted to the point of weakness. His shepherd's crook, which became the "rod of God," is a symbol not only of power and authority but also of discipline. Moses, like the shepherd David, knew that the rod and staff of the Great Shepherd give courage (Ps. 23:4 MOFFATT).

Perhaps it is debatable whether Moses' enraged breaking of the tablets when he descended from the mountain to find his people worshiping the golden calf is a "lapse" in self-control or a justifiable expression of "holy indignation." On one hand, righteous anger over sin is not only justifiable but essential (note that Jehovah does not rebuke Moses' anger), and the broken tablets merely symbolize the already-broken law. On the other hand, the language, at least in some translations, seems to connote an impulsive outburst, a violent outrage resembling Moses' prior and subsequent lapses in control. "Moses *blazed out* in anger; he *flung down* the tablets and broke them . . ." (Exod. 32:30 MOFFATT). We must be wary of excusing as "righteous indignation" those reactions of ours which may in fact be impulsive losses of self-control.

Undoubtedly one of the most serious lapses in Moses' self-discipline came during the forty years of wandering in the wilderness. When the people complained of having no water at Meribah of Kadesh, Jehovah told Moses that he was to speak to the rock and it would then bring forth water. Moses' reaction involved a six-fold offense so serious that God forbade Moses' entrance into the Promised Land. This is what Moses said and did: ''Hear now, ye rebels; must we fetch you water out of this rock? And Moses lifted up his hand, and with his rod he smote the rock twice'' (Num. 20:10–11 KJV).

Moses showed a lack of self-discipline in his peevish and resentful attitude (''must we''); in arrogantly taking the credit for himself and for Aaron (''must *we*''); in speaking unadvisedly (''ye rebels''; cf. Ps. 106:33); in losing his temper (''he smote the rock''); in not trusting the power of God (v. 12); and finally in flagrantly disobeying God's command to *speak* to the rock.

What a tragedy that after all the years of faithful, disciplined service, Moses lost the reward of entering the Promised Land because of this lapse of self-discipline.

OTHER OLD TESTAMENT EXAMPLES OF SELF-DISCIPLINE

The Old Testament provides numerous other examples of people who manifested self-discipline. Especially noteworthy, for example, is Joseph, who maintained his self-control in refusing to lie with Potiphar's wife (Gen. 39) and then endured patiently for years in prison (Gen. 39–41). Later, as governor in Egypt, he showed remarkable control in dealing with his brothers, not seeking revenge for the mistreatment he had received at their hands.

Another illustration is the story of Gideon and his 300 men (Judg. 7). Gideon started with 32,000 men. When those who were afraid were told to go home, 22,000 left. Another test of self-discipline was exacted: those who lapped water like a dog or bowed down on their knees to drink were told to go home—9700 men left. The 300 men who remained were those who showed not only courage but self-discipline. They were chosen to vanquish the 135,000 Midianites.

Other Old Testament figures illustrate the tragedy of lapses into disobedience. Noah, who maintained godly self-discipline for 120 years while building the ark amid the mockery of the people, shamefully lost control after the flood and lay drunken and naked in his tent. Abraham—who displayed such self-discipline in leaving Ur of the Chaldees, in giving Lot the choice land, in interceding for Sodom, in passing the test of faith and obedience even to the point of being willing to sacrifice his son—lied to Abimelech about Sarah and capitulated to Sarah's impatience for a son.

Samson, for all his mighty strength and deeds of valor, was overcome by his tragic flaw: he could control everything and everyone but himself. Similarly, David could defeat Goliath and ten thousands of Philistines, but lost control and committed adultery and murder. And Elijah, just after his mountaintop victory over the 450 prophets of Baal, lost emotional control when he crept under a juniper tree in the wilderness and requested to die.

Have you ever noticed that many, if not most, of our lapses in self-discipline come after moments of great victory and joy? Satan often trips us up in self-indulgence after a great Bible conference or a time of real spiritual blessing.

NEW TESTAMENT EXAMPLES

The New Testament also gives us personal examples of self-discipline or the lack of it. The disciples expressed great resolve to follow Jesus faithfully—only to fall asleep in the Garden. And later that evening they scattered when Jesus was apprehended.

Peter, like so many of us, impulsively expressed allegiance to the Master and then, just as impulsively, denied Him. Peter cut off the ear of the high priest's servant and was sternly rebuked by Jesus (Matt. 26:51–54). After the Crucifixion, Peter precipitately told the others, "I'm going out to fish" (John 21:3), returning to his former style of life. But a self-centered lifestyle leads nowhere. The resurrected Christ establishes love as the only proper motivation for action.

What accounts for the difference between this impetuous, undisciplined Peter and the self-disciplined, miracle-working apostle described in the Book of Acts? It is the same difference that can transform our lives into fruitful servants of God—the power of the Holy Spirit, which works through individuals, controlling faculties and energizing wills. The rushing mighty wind and the tongues as of fire that signaled the Spirit's outpouring on Pentecost symbolized the controlled power of God. The fire that burned in the bush but never consumed it and the fire-like tongues that appeared over each Spirit-filled believer symbolized other things as well: the purging of self-will, the burning away of the dross of self-indulgence, and the flaming forth of authoritative power under control.

6 / Copybook Christianity: Learning Self-Discipline From a Perfect Model

One day Uncle Maury, whose eighty-five years had taught him much about life and the disciplined living of it, made this observation: "One of our problems today is that most people just aren't fit to be entrusted with themselves!"

"Yes," I thought, "we need self-discipline. Our lack of fitness is our inability to control ourselves." But the assertion suggests something further: that we, in ourselves, are inadequate to improve ourselves; we lack sufficient discipline even to commence becoming self-disciplined! To compensate for this human weakness, God provided the dynamic of self-discipline in His Holy Spirit and the model of self-discipline in the person and life of Christ.

Jesus Christ is our perfect example. Peter wrote, "Christ suffered for you, leaving you an example, that you should follow in his footsteps" (1 Peter 2:21). Peter uses two metaphors here to describe Jesus as our example. Both show us in the role of dependent children.

Do you remember when you were learning to write in cursive? Try as you might to reproduce those twenty-six squiggly characters, your awkward, uncoordinated movements produced only embarrassing scrawls. Perhaps you improved when your teacher

67

made the letters for you to trace and copy, or held and steadied your hand as you both went over the letters. This is exactly the picture that Peter gives. The word translated "example" is *hypogrammos,* a line of script a schoolchild copies in imitation, a writing pattern to follow. Jesus is the Word, perfectly structured and exemplary; the indwelling Spirit is our teacher, taking the things of Christ and showing them to us (John 14:26; 16:13–14).

Jesus is also the trailblazer. Hebrews 12:2 can be read: "Looking unto Jesus, the author [trailblazer] and finisher of our faith." As a youngster you may have had the experience of trudging through deep snow by following in the tracks of your parent. In such a way the believer, energized by the Holy Spirit, develops self-discipline by following the example of Christ. "As children copy their fathers you, as God's children, are to copy him," Paul wrote (Eph. 5:1 PHILLIPS).

In that classic work of the fifteenth century, *The Imitation of Christ,* Thomas á Kempis has the master admonish his disciple to be self-disciplined: "My son, take great care to ensure that in every place, action and outward occupation, you remain free and your own master. Control circumstances, and do not allow them to control you. Only so can you be master and ruler of your actions, not their servant or slave, a free man and a true Christian, enjoying the freedom and high destiny of the children of God." Such is the example of Christ.

CHRIST: THE PERFECT MODEL

Have you ever noticed how Christ perfectly exemplifies all the graces of the Spirit mentioned in Galatians 5? Certainly "No one has greater love than the one who lays down his life for his friends" (John 15:13)—and Jesus gave up His life for His enemies! Paul urges us to imitate this high example of *love:* "Live a life of love, following the example of Christ" (Eph. 5:2 TCNT).

Similarly, the writer of the Book of Hebrews tells us that we should be "Looking unto Jesus the author and finisher of our faith; who for the joy that was set before him endured the cross" (12:2 KJV). The word translated "looking unto" is much stronger in the Greek, conveying the idea of regarding fixedly, with undivided attention, by looking *away from* everything else—a disciplined, rather than a distracted, look. One of the supreme lessons to be learned from Christ's example is that a proper motivation and sanction of the disciplined endurance of suffering is the promise of *joy.*

The third grace, *peace,* is such an essential part of the nature of Christ that Isaiah's prophecy, given nearly eight hundred years before Jesus' birth, referred to Christ as the very "Prince of Peace" (9:6). At His birth angels announced peace on earth "among men with whom He is pleased" (Luke 2:14 NASB).

Christ is also the perfect example of *patience,* as Paul says: "I was shown mercy so that in me, the worst of sinners, Christ Jesus might display his unlimited patience as an example for those who would believe on him" (1 Tim. 1:16).

Elsewhere Paul, in defending his apostolic authority, appeals to the Corinthian believers on the basis of "the *gentleness* (or kindness) of Christ" (2 Cor. 10:1 GOODSPEED). Jesus invited all who are weary and overburdened to come, bend their necks to His yoke of discipline, and learn from Him because He is "meek and lowly in heart" (Matt. 11:29 KJV). What greater picture of self-disciplined condescension than that of the mighty King of Kings, the supreme Lord of the universe, "mounted on a donkey, even on a colt, the foal of a beast of burden" (Matt. 21:5 MLB)?

Jesus exemplifies perfect *goodness* even in the midst of a corrupt environment, illustrating self-control over circumstances and environment.

And finally, Jesus exemplifies *faithfulness*—to the Father, to His task of redeeming mankind through His death, to His promises, even to His unbelieving people—despite great difficulty and great opposition from the forces of darkness. "He was faithful to the one who appointed him" (Heb. 3:2); "the one [Jesus] who calls you is faithful and he will do it" (1 Thess. 5:24); "he who promised is faithful" (2 Tim. 2:13). And it is precisely the faithfulness of Christ that enables us to maintain our own self-discipline: "The Lord is faithful, who shall [e]stablish you, and keep you from evil" (2 Thess. 3:3 KJV).

These spiritual graces, all manifested to perfection in the life of Christ, work together, each complementing the others, to produce *self-control,* which, in turn, influences the other eight.

THE SELF-DISCIPLINE OF THE INCARNATION

The self-discipline of Christ is perhaps nowhere more clearly shown than in His incarnation. And this same humble attitude and disciplined mind should be manifest in our lives, Paul says:

> Your attitude should be the same as that of Christ Jesus:
> Who, being in very nature God,
>   did not consider equality with God
>   something to be grasped,
> but made himself nothing,
>   taking the very nature of a servant,
>   being made in human likeness.
> And being found in appearance as a man,
>   he humbled himself
>   and became obedient to death—
>   even death on a cross!
>   (Phil. 2:5–8)

Note the six characteristics of self-discipline exemplified in Jesus' "humbling himself." First, He willingly set aside His rights, His privileges, His prerogatives. To do so requires great self-sacrifice, but should we do less than willingly surrender our rights for His glory? "The student is not above his teacher, nor a servant above his master" (Matt. 10:24). "As you stand in awe of Christ," Paul says, "submit to each other's rights" (Eph. 5:21 KNOX).

How foreign to most of us this submission is, for we insist stubbornly on our "rights," our "just due." "What's the matter with that crazy driver? Doesn't he know *I* have the right-of-way? And man, I'm gonna take it if it's the last thing I do!" "I've been a faithful, loyal member of this church for twelve years, and I guess I've got a right to expect. . . ." "All I want is my rightful share. . . ."

Second, Jesus showed self-discipline in making Himself "of no reputation." He wasn't concerned with His image. He did not say, "Why, I can't become a servant. What would people think?" or "People won't know I'm God if I do that!"

Third, Jesus showed submission in taking upon Himself the form of a slave. Service always demands great discipline. Perhaps this is the reason so few of us are willing to do it. Jesus' service was maintained by inner resources, motivated by the prospect of joy and by love for the Father and for sinful men.

Fourth, His condescension, His disciplined descent, is seen also in His assuming the likeness of men, who the psalmist refers to as being made "a little lower than the angels" (8:5 KJV). In having done so, He is able to "be touched with the feeling of our infirmities . . . in all points [having been] tempted like as we are, yet without sin" (Heb. 4:15 KJV).

The fifth and sixth characteristics of self-discipline have to do with Jesus' death. Not only did He choose to die, but He chose the most ignoble and ignominious form of death conceivable—that of a common criminal. The Son of God, being God, need not have died. He could have stepped back into heaven from the Mount of Transfiguration or, at the very least, He could have died quietly with friends in Bethany. Instead, He disciplined Himself to die an accursed death, "Cursed is everyone who is hanged on a tree" (Gal. 3:13).

JESUS HAD TOTAL SELF-DISCIPLINE

Jesus exemplified perfect self-discipline in all areas of His life. He was disciplined not only mentally, but also physically, emotionally, socially, and spiritually. Luke described Him at the age of twelve: "Jesus grew in wisdom [mentally] and stature [physically], and in favor [emotionally] with God [spiritually] and men [socially]" (Luke 2:52).

Physically

Jesus subjected His body to the discipline of fasting—on one occasion for forty days and nights (Matt. 4:2). He taught His disciples its benefits and, for certain effects such as the exorcism of some demons, its necessity (Matt. 17:21; Mark 9:29).

All three of the recorded temptations of Christ entailed testings of His self-control over His physical nature. First, when He was ravenously hungry, Satan tempted Him to turn stones into bread —a temptation to live by sight rather than by faith. But Jesus resisted with the scriptural principle that the spiritual always takes precedence over the physical, the supernatural over the natural, the eternal over the temporal. Natural, legitimate physical needs, such as hunger, must be satisfied in God's way and in God's own time.

In the second temptation, according to Matthew's account, Satan urged Jesus to test the divine promise of physical protection by jumping from a pinnacle of the temple. But Jesus again resisted Satan's insistence that He test the promises of God.

The third temptation was perhaps the most subtly appealing of all: it was a temptation to do wrong (acquiesce to Satan) for the right reason (reclaim the world for God). Satan tempted Christ to reclaim the world by taking a shortcut (worshiping him) rather than by suffering physical anguish and death on the cross.

Satan tempts us in these same three ways: *indulge* your physical desires, *flaunt* the physical to presume on God's protection, and *spare* yourself physical suffering and pain. Only self-discipline of our physical nature and disciplined use of the Scripture will win the victory for us, as it did for Christ, our Example.

Emotionally

Because He is the God–man, God of very God and man of very man, and was tempted in all areas, just as we are, yet without sin (Heb. 4:15), Jesus manifested all forms of human emotion without losing control. His great love never degenerated into sentimentality or blinded Him to reality. I recently saw a sign that read: "Love is the ultimate drug." But Jesus was never drugged by love, for God's love is genuine.

Jesus found delight in doing the Father's will (Ps. 40:8) and in fulfilling the law of God (Ps. 119). He found joy in enduring the suffering and shame of the cross.

We must be careful not to underestimate the agony, the sorrow, and the extreme depression of Jesus in Gethsemane (Matt. 26:37–38; Mark 14:33–34). But He did not give in to despair; He was not overcome by it. Rather He submitted to the will of the Father. Isaiah described Jesus as "a man of sorrows, acquainted with bitterest grief. . . ." But "it was *our* grief he bore, *our* sorrows that weighed him down" (53:3–4 LB). He wept over Jerusalem (Luke 19:41–44), and He openly wept at Lazarus's grave (John 11:35). But never did Jesus lose the balance between the sorrow and the joy of the mission, between pain and pleasure, between depression and exultation; never did He identify with suffering and defeat to the exclusion of the joy of victory.

Jesus showed concern, but never anxious care or worry. His lifestyle was disciplined but casual because of His trust in the Father. "Foxes have holes and birds of the air have nests, but the Son of Man has no place to lay his head," He told His disciples (Matt. 8:20). He lived what He preached about the cure for anxious care (Matt. 6:25–34).

He also illustrated how to be angry without sinning, as Paul admonishes us in Ephesians 4:26. In purifying the temple of unscrupulous merchandizers, He exemplified holy indignation, even making a whip of cords and driving out the animals and moneychangers (John 2:13–16). We must be careful that we do not justify as "holy indignation" what is really carnal loss of temper resulting from wounded pride. The object of Jesus' legitimate anger was the violation of the sanctity of His Father's house, not violation of Himself. He illustrated that we cannot love as we ought to love unless we hate where we ought to hate.

Our Lord was verbally and physically violated, but His reactions to these abuses were always forbearing, restrained, and loving. For a picture of His genuine self-discipline in action, read Isaiah 50 and 53, the account of the suffering servant. Note especially Jesus' *reactions*. "I gave my back to those who beat me, my cheeks to those who pulled out my beard; I did not hide my face from mocking and spitting" (50:6). There has never been such condescension, such power held in perfect control!

In rebuking Peter for cutting off the ear of the high priest's servant, Jesus says He could have called twelve legions of angels to His aid, but He did not. Here is perfect obedience to the godly trait of blessing those who persecute you, of overcoming evil with good (Rom. 12:14, 21). This kind of self-control cuts against the very grain of our human nature. But would God command us to do something without providing the means by which it can be accomplished? Certainly not, for He has given us a perfect model in the Person of His Son.

Socially

Jesus also provides the perfect example of social and domestic self-discipline. He was submissive to Joseph and Mary: "He went down to Nazareth with them and was obedient to them" (Luke 2:51). Further, He was in subjection to civil authority. He admonished individuals to "Give to Caesar what is Caesar's, and to God what is God's" (Matt. 22:21). He perfectly exemplified the self-disciplined subjection to authority as enjoined by Paul (Rom. 13:1–7) and by Peter (1 Peter 2:13–25).

Spiritually

Jesus could truthfully say what ought to be our ideal: "I seek not to please myself but him who sent me" (John 5:30). Nor was it a grudging submission. The Father's will was His very sustenance (John 4:34). His whole purpose in coming into this world was to carry out the will of the Father (Heb. 10:7).

In Jesus' short life on earth He exemplified the disciplined redeeming of time (Eph. 5:16; Col. 4:5). He was never hurried and harried, yet He was never late; His timing was perfect. When He received word that His friend Lazarus was sick, He tarried for two days. Mary and Martha chided Jesus for not arriving "in time" to heal their brother (John 11:21, 32). But Jesus illustrated that the sole criterion for the disciplined use of time is "that God's Son may be glorified through it" (John 11:4).

In the process of carrying out the Father's will, Jesus resolutely headed toward Jerusalem (Luke 9:51). He set His face "like flint'' (Isa. 50:7), a figure that conveys His resolve and unswerving purpose. Never has there been such a superlative manifestation of cool self-control and calm composure as in the suffering of Christ. Peter, in the passage where he presents Christ as our line of script to imitate, echoes Isaiah's description of the suffering servant: "When they hurled their insults at him, he did not retaliate; when he suffered, he made no threats" (1 Peter 2:23). Under the severest of provocation, He manifested the ultimate in restraint, in submission, in quiet forbearance.

Jesus' self-control is shown especially in His silences. Perhaps it is more difficult to remain silent in the face of personal affront and provocation than it is to speak out in defense of a challenged cause. Before the false accusations of the chief priests and elders, Jesus remained silent; before the interrogation of Pilate, Jesus answered not a word (Matt. 27:12–14). When He spoke, it was said that "No one ever spoke the way this man does" (John 7:46), for He possessed a tongue that was well-trained (Isa. 50:4). When He spoke, His disciplined words, seasoned with the salt of grace, were filled with transcendent wisdom, but no less did He manifest His discipline by the strength of His silences.

Perhaps most amazing of all is Christ's self-discipline in willing His own death, even though His enemies thought the event to be in their own hands. "I lay down my life," He told His disciples. "No one takes it from me, but I lay it down of my own accord. . . . I have authority to take it again" (John 10:17–18). How often in our lives, too, it appears that the forces of evil are in control, whereas all the while He, working in and through us, is the center of control!

Underlying the disciplined will, heart, body, and mind is the disciplined spirit. Lacking disciplined devotion, none can lay claim to a genuinely self-disciplined life. This is why the secular, humanistic self-help books on "how to take control of your life" are ultimately ineffective. They overlook or ignore an indispensable dimension—the spiritual. Again, Jesus is the perfect model. Mark tells us that "in the morning, rising up a great while before day, he went out and departed into a solitary place, and there prayed'' (1:35). Later Jesus sent the disciples away and went into the mountain to pray. Similarly, Luke writes that Jesus went into the hills and prayed all night long (6:12).

Do we have the kind of self-discipline manifested by Jesus? Impossible, you say? Certainly it is—in our own strength. That's why human resolutions and fleshly attempts at self-discipline are doomed to failure. But we must not forget the promise Jesus made to every one who believes on Him: ''Greater works than these shall he do'' (John 14:12) because He was going to the Father and sending the Holy Spirit to empower every believer. To what did Jesus attribute His victory? ''The Spirit of the Lord is on me,'' He said (Luke 4:18).

Indwelling every believer is the self-same Spirit who empowered the perfectly disciplined Christ. The Spirit of Him who raised up Christ from the dead gives life to our mortality (Rom. 8:11), enabling us to master our circumstances. The same grace—*charis* (that which serves to transform unpleasing circumstances into pleasing ones)—which enabled Christ to transform death to life, despair to hope, and chaos to order is available to every believer today.

Someone may be thinking, ''Sure, that's all very good, this talk about Christ as the model of self-discipline. But He was God, and since God is the very essence of order, how could Jesus fail to be perfectly self-disciplined? But we're mortals with an evil nature, and we fail all the time!'' It's true. As mortals, we fail when we operate in the flesh. But we have available to us the same source of victory Jesus had. We must appropriate it as He did. As God, He was not able to fail, but as a man He was able *not* to fail. As God, He was not able to be undisciplined, but as a man He was able *not* to be undisciplined. And by following His example, energized by the same Spirit and appropriating the same divine grace, we too are able *not* to be undisciplined.

DISCIPLINE OF THE WHOLE SELF

7 / The Christian's Daily Dozen: The Disciplined Spirit

"Get control of yourself!" an exasperated father shouts at his son. "Pull yourself together!" says friend to friend. "Shape up and get on the stick!" harried teacher reproaches student. "Get with it!" spouse urges spouse. And so it goes. "One of these days I'll get it all together," we promise ourselves. But where do we begin? And how?

There is, of course, no magic wafer which, if swallowed, will produce instant self-control. Christian self-discipline is part of the fruit of the Spirit, but fruit trees must be cultivated, nurtured, pruned, and allowed to mature—a process which requires time and deliberate effort.

In the process of growing fruit, there is a definite starting point when the seed is planted. Then, given the right conditions, it germinates, sprouts, and grows into a tree capable of bearing fruit. Similarly, genuine spiritual self-discipline must begin somewhere, sometime. It doesn't just happen. *Christian* self-discipline must begin with the seed of the gospel springing up unto salvation.

The beginning of self-mastery is to be mastered by Christ, to yield to His lordship. "Wouldst thou have thy flesh obey thy spirit?" Augustine asked. "Then let thy spirit obey thy God. Thou must be governed, that thou may'st govern."

SELF-DISCIPLINE INVOLVES THE WHOLE SELF

Genuine self-discipline necessarily involves the whole person, all of our faculties. Our being created in the image of God means, among other things, that we are fashioned after the pattern of God's triunity. The Godhead consists of God the Father, God the Son, and God the Holy Spirit; human personhood consists of soul, body, and spirit. Paul prayed that God would sanctify the Thessalonians wholly, completely, through and through and that their "whole spirit, soul and body [might] be kept blameless" (1 Thess. 5:23). Similarly, the divine ideal is that we become self-disciplined in all three areas.

The spirit is that part of us that permits awareness of God and communion with Him. The soul constitutes the very seat of our personality, which is comprised of intellect, emotions, and will. The body, of course, includes our physical being, our senses and sensations. Or to express it in another way, the spirit is God-conscious, the soul is self-conscious, and the body is world-conscious.

THE FACULTIES OF PERSONHOOD

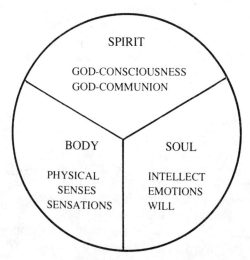

One *truly* can be self-disciplined only if *all three areas* are engaged. An individual who strives to control a violent temper or who works hard at losing weight is dealing with only a part of the human personhood; therefore, regardless of the degree of success, he or she cannot lay claim to genuine self-discipline. The spiritual dimension of this life is missing or dormant. It does not seem valid to speak of "partial discipline" because the human faculties are so closely interrelated that their intimate, mutual actions and reactions are all but indiscernible. Are we not told that only the living, powerful Word of God is able to "pierce even to the severance of soul and spirit" (Heb. 4:12 MOFFATT)?

The person who is spiritually dead or the believer who ignores or neglects the spiritual side of his or her nature is incapable of experiencing self-discipline as it is presented in the Scripture. The law itself is spiritual (Rom. 7:14), and therefore no carnal effort to achieve perfection can ever succeed.

THE FACULTIES OF THE UNREGENERATE PERSON

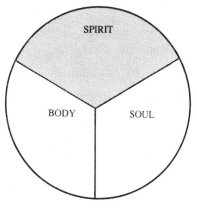

The individual whose spirit is dead in sin or unyielded to the Spirit may at times achieve certain limited curbs and controls that may appear to be self-discipline. But with one entire dimension of personhood uninvolved, genuine self-discipline is impossible.

Surely this is one of the reasons for the frustration of Benjamin

Franklin in his project of self-discipline which he described in his *Autobiography:*

> I would conquer all that either natural inclination, custom, or company might lead me into. As I knew, or thought I knew, what was right or wrong, I did not see why I might not *always* do the one and avoid the other. But I soon found I had undertaken a task of more difficulty than I had imagined. While my attention was taken up and care employed in guarding against one fault, I was often surprised by another. Habit took advantage of inattention. Inclination was sometimes too strong for reason.

Though he admittedly borrowed the plan and methodology of self-inventory from the great Puritan, Cotton Mather, Franklin essentially failed in his noble project for several reasons. He was a nonspiritual man attempting to develop spiritual virtues through mere resolution and human strength. Such an attempt is like trying to grow fruit without a tree!

Can you imagine such a dialogue as this?

"Gr-r-r-u-u-u-nt. Gr-o-o-o-a-a-a-n. Str-r-r-a-a-ain."

"Hey, fella. Whatcha doin there?"

"Gr-r-r-u-u-unt. Why, I'm producing fruit. The fruit of moderation and sincerity and order and frugality and . . . and . . ."

"But don'tcha hafta have a tree to produce fruit?"

"Str-r-r-a-a-ain. A tree? Who needs a tree when ya got determination? Oh, but I *do* have this branch from a friend's orange tree."

"Say, could I sample one of your oranges?"

"Gr-o-o-o-a-a-a-n. Orange? Oh! Well, I don't have any *yet.* But I'm working on it."

"No oranges? Well, how about a little tangelo? No? A kumquat then? Not even a kumquat? Say, fella, don'tcha think ya better go plant a fruit tree?"

The incomplete, spiritually dead person can be holy only when *made* whole (the words *holy* and *whole* are derived from the same Old English word) by being filled with the Spirit of God.

SELF-DISCIPLINE BEGINS WITH SPIRIT CONTROL

Where does one begin then in one's desire to be self-disciplined? The only logical place to begin is with the Holy Spirit working through *our* spirits, that part of us that is God-conscious, that permits our awareness of God and our communion with Him.

For the unbeliever this means repentance, receiving Christ as Savior and being made spiritually alive. For the believer it means continuous commitment and cleansing and continuous filling by the Spirit, submitting to the lordship of Christ.

Paul describes contrasting lifestyles. He admonishes us to "be not drunk with wine, wherein is excess; but keep on being filled with the Spirit" (Eph. 5:18 KJV). A person controlled by alcoholic spirits loses control and acts in an unrestrained and unbecoming manner; a Spirit-filled person yields control to God and acts in a manner that is disciplined and becoming.

To be filled with the Spirit is not to possess *more* of the Spirit, for He indwells every believer in all of His fullness (cf. Rom. 8:9; 1 Cor. 6:19); rather, the Spirit possesses more of the believer, exercising full control over his or her faculties. When the Holy Spirit masters the human spirit, it, in turn, is able to master the soul (the seat of our personality and the part of us that is self-conscious) and body (that part of us that is world-conscious). According to the remainder of Ephesians 5, evidence of the Spirit's control is praise, rejoicing, thanksgiving, and self-controlled submission in relationships.

"The spirit indeed is willing," Jesus said, "but the flesh is weak" (Matt. 26:41). That is, the human spirit of the believer is providing the genuine, enduring motivation for self-discipline, because it has been brought under the control of God's Spirit.

The believer should experience daily, even hourly, cleansing, filling, and yielding to the Spirit. But more than submission to the Spirit's control is necessary; in fact, it is only the beginning. It is necessary to *walk* in the Spirit, to maintain a disciplined devotional life—every day. To have a disciplined spirit, the believer needs his or her spiritual daily dozen.

Daily Prayer

Several years ago my wife and I visited the Wesley residence in London. The guide pointed out a small upstairs bedroom which was used as a prayer room by John and Charles and by their godly mother, Susanna. The floorboards had been worn smooth by their knees as they knelt in prayer—regularly, daily.

What does discipline have to do with praying? Just a little bit of everything. Self-discipline is both a cause and effect of prayer. Without spiritual self-discipline we do not really pray. Peter urges believers, in view of the end time, to ''be clear-minded and self-controlled so that you can pray'' (1 Peter 4:7). Moffatt renders the verse: ''Steady then; keep cool and pray.'' That's not bad advice, is it? Keep cool—steady, collected, self-controlled—for the purpose of prayer.

But how can we *get* cool and *stay* that way in such a frantic world as this? Would you believe through prayer? ''We can really pray only when we are self-controlled, but we become self-controlled through prayer?'' you say. Right. It's a gracious circle. Self-discipline is a fruit of the Spirit, as we have seen, but it must be cultivated and developed, just as a measure of faith is given to every person (Rom. 12:3) but at the same time faith ''comes from hearing the message, and the message is heard through the word of Christ'' (Rom. 10:17).

Disciplined praying is praying that is at once in the Spirit and with the human spirit. It is effectual and fervent, persistent and unceasing, full of faith and faithful. (Eph. 6:18; 1 Cor. 14:15; James 5:16; Luke 11:8; 1 Thess. 5:17; James 5:15; Luke 18:1). Disciplined prayer that disciplines the spirit is regular, consistent —daily. The psalmist repeatedly refers to his calling upon the Lord daily (Ps. 86:3), and Daniel's daily prayers sent him to the lion's den. Such dedication in one's prayer life requires and produces discipline of spirit.

Daily Praise

With prayer must come daily, disciplined praise. ''Daily shall he be praised,'' the psalmist writes (Ps. 72:15). Or better yet, ''Seven times a day I praise you'' (119:164). Disciplined praise, like disciplined prayer, is essentially an attitude, a mind-set, a lifestyle, so that David could say, ''From the rising of the sun unto the going down of the same the Lord's name is to be praised" (Ps. 113:3 KJV) and "I will bless the Lord *at all times*: his praise shall *continually* be in my mouth" (34:1 KJV).

"Continually? At all times? That may have worked for David in the Old Testament, but for me, now, in the twentieth century? With a boss like mine? You've got to be kidding!" No, David wasn't kidding, nor was Paul when he listed the giving of thanks "*always* for *all* things" as one of the results of being filled with the Spirit (Eph. 5:20). It's easy to praise God when the sun shines and people smile, but it requires Spirit-motivated discipline to praise God when the rain pours and the boss roars and inflation soars!

At such times we need the kind of spiritual discipline manifested by Samuel Sewall, the American Puritan businessman who, having prayed for spiritual renewal, made this diary entry on June 16, 1707:

> My house was broken open in two places, and about 20 lbs. of plate stolen away, and some linen; my spoon and knife and neckcloth was taken. I said, Is not this an answer to prayer? . . . I say Welcome Christ!

To the spiritually uninitiated person, this may sound like sheer madness. In a similar vein, Paul made a triumphant statement that may appear nothing short of masochistic to some people: "Most gladly therefore will I glory in my infirmities. . . . I take pleasure in infirmities" (2 Cor. 12:9–10). But it is God's Spirit who gives our spirits victory so that we can praise Him continually.

Daily Commitment-Keeping

David spoke of a related daily spiritual discipline: "So will I sing praise unto thy name for ever, that I may daily perform my vows" (Ps. 61:8 KJV). A self-disciplined person keeps promises, even when keeping them is no longer a personal advantage. This passage and others throughout the Old Testament stress the importance of keeping our word, of following through in doing what we promise, not only to God but also to other people. Our greatest ability is dependability, someone has well said. If you say you're going to be somewhere at a certain time, are you there—on time?

A major part of our Christian testimony is the keeping of our commitments, following through on our promises. God has convicted me frequently about this matter—in fact, as recently as last week. In the middle of leading an adult discussion on commitment, my conscience said, "Sure, you get up there and talk about commitment, but did you follow through on your promise to help John move, to check on that book for Pat, to pray for Fred, to visit Frank at the hospital?" I had no alibi. I could only ask forgiveness and power to keep my commitments in the future.

Daily Bible Study

A fourth kind of daily spiritual discipline is the reading, memorizing, and studying of the Scriptures. The believers in Berea "were finer spirits" than the believers in Thessalonica, for they received Paul's preaching with "great eagerness and examined the Scriptures every day to see if what Paul said was true" (Acts 17:11). The word translated "examined" conveys the idea of scrutinizing intensely, weighing, sifting, appraising, and discerning carefully. Paul uses the same verb to characterize the typical activity of the truly "spiritual" person: "He that is spiritual *discerns* all things, yet he himself is discerned of no man" (1 Cor. 2:15).

And why is the spiritual person "discerned of no man"? Because this person is "discerned" by the very Scriptures *he* or *she* discerns: "The word of God is living and active . . . it judges [discerns] the thoughts and attitudes of the heart" (Heb. 4:12). The Word of God serves to discipline our spirits. When we daily examine the Scriptures, those living words in turn examine our own spirits. Again a gracious circle is established: as we discipline our spirits to study the Scriptures, the Scriptures discipline our spirits.

Those who are disciplined in spirit hunger and thirst after righteousness and, as our Lord promised, shall be filled and perfectly satisfied (Matt. 5:6), but not satiated or glutted so that they lose their taste for the things of God. When I was a boy we called this gorging to the point of distaste being "fed out." My parents had a huge strawberry patch, and by the end of the season most of us children were "fed out" on berries. Now obviously no one can get too much of the Word of God, but it is possible for our taste to become dulled through sporadic reading, misreading, and lack of appropriate application and spiritual exercise. It is all too common for us to become weary in and of well-doing. A truly self-disciplined spirit prevents this, motivates us to search the Scriptures regularly, thus further enhancing our spiritual self-discipline.

Have you ever realized that the only place *success* is mentioned in the Bible is in connection with daily meditation on the Scriptures? When Joshua assumed command of the Israelites after the death of Moses, he gave them this secret: "This book of the law shall not depart out of thy mouth; but thou shalt *meditate therein day and night* that thou mayest observe to do according to all that is written therein: for then thou shalt make thy way prosperous, and then shalt thou have good success" (Josh. 1:8 KJV).

The success of our self-discipline will be determined to a large degree by the quantity and quality of Bible study and prayer. If you don't have a regular time set aside each day, why not begin or improve your program of self-discipline with this important step? At first it might be just ten or fifteen minutes a day. You might wish to follow the increasingly popular and helpful *Daily Walk,* a systematic plan for reading the Bible through in one year.[1] Choose the most suitable time of day for you and faithfully keep that appointment with the Lord. But don't become guilt-ridden and demoralized if you miss, as we all do occasionally. If you can, with God's help, win the battle of discipline at this crucial point, it will spur you on in the other areas of your life.

Daily Self-Denial

To be genuinely self-disciplined one must become a disciple of Jesus, who set down this exacting requirement: "If anyone

---

[1]Information can be secured from Walk Thru the Bible Ministries, Inc., P.O. Box 720653, Atlanta, GA 30328.

chooses to be my disciple, he must say 'No' to self, put the cross on his shoulders daily, and continue to follow me'' (Luke 9:23 WILLIAMS). Haven't all of us, like Henderson, the protagonist in Saul Bellow's novel *Henderson the Rain King,* heard a voice within us speaking constantly?

> *I want, I want, I want!* . . . It only said one thing, *I want, I want!* . . . At times I would treat it like an ailing child whom you offer rhymes or candy. I would walk it, I would trot it. I would sing to it or read to it. No use.

No, it's no use to pamper it, cater to it. That will not make it go away. There's nothing to be done but renounce it and consign it to the Cross until we hear only *"God wants."* Discipline of the spirit makes the difference.

Daily Dying

Closely related to daily self-denial is Paul's expression about daily death: ''I die every day'' he said in his great resurrection discourse (1 Cor. 15:31). He faced death every day of his life—whether in fighting the wild beasts in the arena at Ephesus or in severe beatings, stonings, and shipwreck. In his second letter to the Corinthians, Paul again says, ''Every day we experience something of the death of Jesus (4:10 PHILLIPS).

We, too, are daily exposed to death—not on a cross or in a Greek arena or Roman prison, but perhaps within tons of metal soaring through the air or hurtling down a concrete strip. ''Treading change with savage heel,/We must live or die by steel,'' a modern poet puts it. Truly, ''in the midst of life, we are in death.'' But that grim fact, rightly viewed, can serve to discipline us to deeper, more meaningful living.

John Donne, the English poet, reportedly kept on his writing desk a portrait of himself in his shroud so he would be sober-minded and disciplined. We need not go to such morbid extremes, but in addition to dying daily to the old nature, we need to keep before us the real possibility of imminent physical death. This sobering reality can stimulate us to greater self-discipline.

Daily Renewal

In the same passage where Paul talks about this daily exposure to death, he encourages us not to lose heart, for "though outwardly we are wasting away, yet inwardly *we are being renewed day by day*" (2 Cor. 4:16). "Every day the inward man receives fresh strength" (PHILLIPS). This promise is at the heart of spiritual discipline. Unless our spirits are refreshed and strengthened daily, self-discipline in other areas is sure to break down sooner or later.

After David had lost control and committed adultery with Bathsheba, he prayed for spiritual renewal: "Put a new, steadfast spirit in me . . . give me a willing spirit as my strength, that I may teach offenders how thou dealest, till sinful men turn back to thee" (Ps. 51:10, 13 MOFFATT). A renewed spirit produces a self-disciplined spirit, which in turn results in disciplined service.

But how does this daily renewal come about? Isaiah provides the answer: "They that wait upon the Lord shall renew their strength; they shall mount up with wings as eagles; they shall run and not be weary; and they shall walk and not faint" (40:31 KJV). To "wait" in this context does not mean to sit passively with hands folded. The Hebrew word conveys the idea of conscious, disciplined attention, active meditation upon the things of God, who says that spiritual renewal lies "only in returning to me and waiting for me" (Isa. 30:15 LB). Our strength lies in staying quiet before Him. David says much the same thing: "Wait on the Lord: be of good courage, and he shall strengthen thine heart: wait, I say, on the Lord" (Ps. 27:14 KJV).

The impulsive way is often easier than waiting. It takes spiritual self-discipline to be still without being passive and sluggish. In his poem "On His Blindness," John Milton conveys this idea of active waiting: "They also serve who only stand and wait." The secret of renewal, then, goes something like this: the indwelling Spirit, as we yield to Him, produces the fruit of self-discipline, which motivates us daily to wait upon the Lord, and this active devotion in turn reinforces the discipline of our spirits.

Daily Fellowship

Another exercise of spiritual discipline is daily fellowship with God and fellow believers. Of the early church it was said, "Daily they frequented the temple together" (Acts 2:46 MLB). The verb used here conveys the idea of perseverance and unremitting continuance. The same word appears in verse 42, where we are told that the believers "persevered in the apostles' teaching and fellowship, in breaking of bread and in prayers." The word appears again in Ephesians 6:18 to describe intercessory prayer: "Praying always with all prayer and supplication in the Spirit, and watching thereunto with all perseverance and supplication for all saints" (KJV).

The first-century believers met daily to pray, to praise God, to eat together, and to build each other up in the faith. They knew the real meaning of Christian fellowship.

"Hold on!" you say. "Sunday morning church is about all I can manage. I'm just too busy to attend Bible study and the fellowship group and the morning prayer sessions." But to persevere and continue steadfastly, even when it's difficult, is the way of a disciplined spirit: "I've got that important business meeting at 7:30, but I'll drop by the 6:00 prayer meeting and Bible study. It'll put me in the right frame of mind."

Daily Encouragement

One of the results of such disciplined fellowship is that believers are edified through exhortation. This daily encouraging and comforting is yet another exercise of the self-disciplined spirit: "Exhort one another *daily* . . . lest any of you be hardened through the deceitfulness of sin" (Heb. 3:13 KJV). Believers should "help one another to stand firm in the faith every day" (PHILLIPS). This passage suggests that we are not only to develop discipline in our own spirits but also to assist in the development of self-discipline in fellow believers.

The word translated "exhort" is *parakaleo*, from which *paraclete*, a scriptural description of the Holy Spirit, is derived. Isn't it interesting that when we are disciplined in our spirits by the Spirit, we serve a function which is an extension of the Spirit's function? God "comforteth [the same word *parakaleo*] us in all our tribulation, that we may be able to comfort them which are in any trouble, by the comfort wherewith we ourselves are comforted of God" (2 Cor. 1:4 KJV). This is spiritual self-discipline in action—and multiplied!

It's easy to see how exhortation, especially daily exhortation, could either flag in the face of opposition or flair into bitter criticism. What prevents it from doing so? Self-discipline *of* the spirit *by* the Spirit. Paul urges young Timothy to "reprove, rebuke, exhort with all longsuffering and doctrine" (2 Timothy 4:2 KJV). The word translated "longsuffering" conveys the idea of utmost self-discipline, being unflagging and inexhaustible in patience.

What do we ordinarily talk about with fellow believers, even when we see them at church? The weather? Last night's football game? The kids? The high cost of living? Or do we share spiritual victories and struggles? Wouldn't we be shocked if our old question, "How are you?" were answered with: "I'm not well—spiritually. I pray but don't hear an answer. I've been constantly defeated this week"? Or when was the last time we said or heard a rejoicing response, such as: "I'm praising the Lord for what He's done for me this past week. Let me share it with you . . ."? Exhortation such as this does not come from talking about the weather—unless we're talking about the Lord's showers of blessings!

Daily Witnessing

If daily encouragement of fellow believers is one manifestation of a self-disciplined spirit, a reasonable witness to unbelievers is another. On his visit to Athens, Paul "was reasoning in the synagogue with the Jews and the God-fearing Gentiles, and in the market place *every day* with those who happened to be present" (Acts 17:17 NASB). Again, at Ephesus Paul spent three months reasoning and persuading in the synagogue and two full years "reasoning daily in the school of Tyrannus." The result was that "all who lived in Asia heard the word of the Lord" (Acts 19:9–10 NASB). Paul's witness for the Lord was not sporadic and hit-and-miss, but regular and daily.

We, too, are commanded to "always be prepared to give an answer to everyone who asks you to give the reason for the hope that you have," but we are to do it "with gentleness and respect" (1 Peter 3:15–16). This readiness to reason, in a cautious and courteous manner, is borne of spiritual self-discipline. Without it, we may alienate and repulse an unbeliever. We may win the argument, but lose the soul.

Daily Giving

The regular, systematic meeting of the material needs of fellow believers is also important. In the first century church, there was *daily* distribution of food (Acts 6:1). When the church grew and expanded throughout Judea and Samaria, seven Spirit-filled deacons were appointed to administer the distribution. Christians today should be no less systematic in regularly ministering to the physical needs of others.

Pious platitudes do not feed hungry people. Patting the needy person on the shoulder and saying, "There, there," is not enough. James condemned such inaction: "Suppose a brother or sister is without clothes and daily food. If one of you says to him, 'Go, I wish you well; keep warm and well fed,' but does nothing about his physical needs, what good is it?" (2:15–16).

A young couple in my church, who had their own children to support, weren't content to click their tongues, "Tsk, Tsk," over the starving Cambodians; they took three needy individuals into their home. Not everyone is able to do this, but we can do *something*. At Christmas, for example, you can seek out a family less fortunate than yours and buy them food and gifts. Our family has been doing this ever since our boys were small—and it's a blessing none of us would think of missing.

Being a hearer *and* a doer demands a self-disciplined spirit. Often giving and sharing demand sacrifice: maybe keeping the old car a while longer, doing without those new golf clubs, postponing plans for that trip to Hawaii. But isn't this one of the acid tests of our Christian commitment? James reminds us that "Pure religion and undefiled before God and the Father is this: To visit the fatherless and widows in their affliction, and to keep [ourselves] unspotted from the world" (1:27 KJV).

Daily Vigilance

The last of the believer's daily dozen exercises for a disciplined spirit is continuous, vigilant watching. Proverbs 8:34 says: "Happy is the man listening to me, *watching daily* at my gates, keeping watch at my doorposts" (MLB). To "watch daily" at the gates of wisdom means that we constantly should be aware of what is going on. We should be sharp and alert, not mentally and spiritually sluggish, benighted, or provincial, for such is not a sign of piety.

Jesus enjoined His followers to watchfulness: "Take ye heed, watch and pray: for ye know not when the time is. . . . Watch ye, therefore: for ye know not when the master of the house cometh. . . . Lest coming suddenly he find you sleeping. And what I say unto you I say unto all, Watch" (Mark 13:33–37 KJV). Luke's record of these words makes the failure to watch and be ready clearly associated with *lack* of self-discipline: "Take heed to yourselves, lest at any time your hearts be overcharged with surfeiting [self-indulgence], and drunkenness, and the cares of this life, and so that day come upon you unawares" (Luke 21:34).

To watch also means to be on our guard, to have our defensive and offensive weapons always ready. Paul urges believers to "Be on your guard; stand firm in the faith; be men of courage; be strong. Do everything in love" (1 Cor. 16:13).

Paul further admonishes believers in the last days to keep awake, alert, watchful, cautious and on their guard and self-controlled. Those of the night, those who are self-indulgent, sleep on, but we, who belong to the day, should control ourselves (1 Thess. 5:6, 8). Are you and I daily watching for wisdom, daily watching for the Lord's return, daily watching out for Satan's wily strategies? Or are we spiritually sluggish and dull?

Perhaps Paul summarizes the point best when he urges young Timothy to watch in all things, to be self-controlled always—to keep his head (2 Tim. 4:5).

We'll learn in the next chapter what *kind* of a head (mind) to keep. But in order to have a truly self-disciplined mind, we need a self-disciplined spirit. In a real sense, genuine self-discipline is not only a fruit of the *Spirit* but also a fruit of the *spirit*. And God has made abundant provision for it through the believer's daily dozen.

8 / Renovating the Ruined Palace: The Disciplined Mind

Imagine, if you can, a giant computer the size of the Empire State Building, towering 102 stories or 1250 feet into the air. Within its intricate system, billions of electronic circuits hum; huge magnetic core cylinders rotate, storing information and compiling output data; zeroes and ones alternate and combine with sophisticated precision. But suddenly the control panel flashes a warning: the central processing unit malfunctions, reels of tape spin erratically, output data is distorted. For all its impressive design, this mechanical marvel is simply a unit out of control—and as such it fails to serve the purpose for which it was created.

The human mind is rather like this computer. Scientists have estimated that if a computer capable of performing the functions of the human brain could be built, it would have to be at least the size of the Empire State Building. Of course the brain is far more complex and efficient than any computer, and the mind, part of the human soul, is much more than the gray matter of the brain.

Our ability to think, reason, and reflect is a special gift of God—a part of what it means to be created uniquely in the image of God. A student in one of my classes argued most insistently that *her* horse and dog possess not just instinct but reasoning ability as well. But the psalmist sees things differently: "Do not behave like horse or mule, unreasoning creatures, whose course must be checked with bit and bridle'' (32:9 NEB). The point is that God guides us through our understanding, and it is the mind that is instrumental in controlling our behavior and curbing our appetites. Consequently, as John R. W. Stott has noted in his booklet *Your Mind Matters,* ''self-control is primarily mind-control.''

Before disobedience caused the Fall in Eden, the human mind was harmoniously in tune with the divine Mind and therefore perfectly ordered and controlled. But sin alienated the human mind from God, darkened the intellect, and introduced mental disorder and lack of intellectual discipline. Paul says that the unregenerate have minds ''clouded with darkness'' (KNOX); they are alienated from the life of God ''because ignorance prevails among them and their minds have grown hard as stone'' (Eph. 4:17 NEB). Before we were redeemed we were *''enemies in mind by wicked works''* (Col. 1:21).

The human mind was ''once a fair and stately palace'' ruled by ''monarch Thought,'' says Edgar Allan Poe's poem ''The Haunted Palace.'' But ''evil things . . . assailed the monarch's high estate'' so that now ''vast forms . . . move fantastically/To a discordant melody.'' Satan, the prince of disorder, and his hosts of angels, now work in and through that fallen palace. The ''lute's well-tuned law'' has changed to discord and confusion.

WHICH COMES FIRST—A DISCIPLINED MIND OR DISCIPLINED THOUGHTS?

There are many who believe that control can be regained through human effort and that order can be restored by cleaning up the rubble and doing some interior decorating. Any consideration of mental discipline must deal initially with this crucial question: Do we achieve a disciplined mind by thinking disciplined thoughts or do we think disciplined thoughts because we have a disciplined mind? Sounds vaguely reminiscent of something about poultry or eggs coming first, doesn't it?

In his book *That Incredible Christian,* A. W. Tozer wrote: ''To be heavenly-minded we must think heavenly thoughts. . . .

God must have all our thoughts if we would experience the sanctification of our minds.'' Does this mean that if we have heavenly thoughts (and what precisely *are* those?) long enough (how long? five years? ten? twenty? fifty?), we one day acquire a heavenly mind (and just what *is that?*)? And does possessing a heavenly mind mean we are of no earthly good?

Undoubtedly there is some truth in what Tozer says, but the point needs a considerable amount of qualification. First, it is important to realize that disciplined, or heavenly, thoughts simply cannot be produced by an undisciplined, or unheavenly, mind. Jesus Himself made this principle clear: "Every good tree bears good fruit, but a bad tree bears bad fruit. A good tree cannot bear bad fruit, and a bad tree cannot bear good fruit" (Matt. 7:17–18). According to Jesus, the criterion for appraisal is the fruit. Solomon makes the thought processes the very indicator of moral character: "As he thinketh in his heart, so is he" (Prov. 23:7 KJV). What do you think about in your unguarded moments? When you're riding in the car or just before you fall off to sleep at night? Are they unrestrained thoughts of self-indulgence—lust of the flesh, conniving thoughts of covetousness and greed, impulses of scorn and hatred? Surely the fact that all of us all too often have such thoughts underscores the fact that we all need self-disciplined minds.

If an undisciplined mind can never produce truly disciplined thoughts, then the solution would obviously lie in achieving a disciplined mind. Right? Can't the disordered, haunted palace be cleaned up, straightened up, tidied up—set in order? The answer is "No."

"No? Why not? We'll get our work crews in there to sweep and scrub and polish and refurbish and, and. . . . What we need is a lot of positive thinking and. . . ."

Sorry, but it just won't work. Jesus told of a house, vacated by an unclean spirit, which was made perfectly straight and clean (Luke 11:25). A perfect picture of a self-disciplined personage, right? Wrong. Jesus said that the unclean spirit joined with seven other demons even more wicked than himself and returned to dwell in the house. And the final state of the man was far worse than the first.

Jesus is not simply saying that self-reformation is utterly futile, which it is. Nor that an empty, idle mind is the devil's workshop, which it is. But that nothing less than an entirely new palace under new ownership and management will do.

The Scripture teaches that there are two distinct, diametrically opposite kinds of minds: the carnal mind, or the mind of the flesh, and the spiritual mind, the mind of Christ. Note what Paul says of these two minds: "People who are controlled by the physical think of what is physical, and people who are controlled by the spiritual think of what is spiritual" (Rom. 8:5 GOODSPEED).

Paul goes on to say that the carnal mind of a sinful man "is death. But the mind controlled by the Spirit is life and peace, because the sinful mind is hostile to God. It does not submit to God's law, *nor can it do so*" (Rom. 8:6–7). Because the mind of the flesh cannot submit to the laws of God, it can never be truly disciplined. The old palace, though swept, polished, and refurbished, is still haunted by those vast forms of evil.

God has made provision for that palace to be completely renovated, made totally new. You and I, the moment we received Christ as Savior and became God's children, received the mind of Christ, the very understanding and intellectual conception of Christ Himself. "We have the mind of Christ," Paul writes fellow believers (1 Cor. 2:16). And in Christ "are hidden all the treasures of wisdom and knowledge" (Col. 2:3). Amazing truth!

WHAT KIND OF MIND IS YOURS?

Have you ever thought about the kind of mind you, as a believer, have? Sounds like a rather circular process, doesn't it— thinking, *with* your mind obviously, *about* your mind? But it's not a futile spiral, for only when we realize what we have can we use what we've got.

Paul tells young Timothy about the kind of mind God has given us: "For God hath not given us the spirit of fear; but of power, and of love, and of a *sound mind*" (2 Tim. 1:7 KJV). It's interesting and significant that the Greek word translated "of a sound mind" *(sophronismos)* is sometimes rendered "self-restraint," "self-control," or "self-discipline." Forms of the word, usually translated "sober" or "soberminded," are popular with Paul, who establishes the trait as a qualification of those who minister the Word (Titus 1:8; 2:2, 4–6). The same word is used in 1 Peter 4:7: "Be clear-minded and self-controlled so that you can pray." Here the word conveys a calm vigor of mind, in short, a well-disciplined mind.

THE DEMONIAC WAS TOTALLY OUT OF CONTROL

Both Mark and Luke use the same word in their accounts of Jesus casting out the legion of demons at Gergesa. Here we have a vivid demonstration of the two minds. Note the before–after picture. When Jesus arrived, He was met by a man mentally, spiritually, physically, and emotionally out of control. Here is the carnal mind with a vengeance! This man dwelt, appropriately, among the tombs. Not only did he lack self-discipline—he could not even be controlled by others. "No one could bind him any more, not even with a chain. For he had often been chained hand and foot, but he tore the chains apart and broke the irons on his feet. No one was strong enough to subdue him" (Mark 5:3–4). An extreme case? Yes, but there's a basic principle here that makes this case illustrative of every carnal mind: When Satan is in control, the human mind is out of control and, like the giant computer or the ruined palace, it is thwarted from its purpose of creation.

The demoniac's practice of "shrieking and mangling himself with sharp stones" (WEYMOUTH) sounds almost like a parody of humanity's futile attempt to achieve self-discipline through asceticism. Nothing but the power of Christ would work then, or today.

Note the "after" picture. When the townspeople came out, they saw the man who had been possessed of a legion of demons sitting, dressed, "and in his right mind," *(sophronounta)*—

perfectly sane (Mark 5:15). Here is a perfectly self-disciplined mind. He instantly, unquestionably obeyed when Jesus sent him to proclaim in his own country the great things that Jesus had done for him. But what of his fellow countrymen? The fact that they were awe-struck by sanity and preferred having their herds of swine to the Savior suggests that the demoniac's was not the only undisciplined mind.

GOD WANTS US TO HAVE A CERTAIN FRAME OF MIND

Does it mean, then, that once a person receives a spiritual mind, his thoughts are perfectly disciplined ever thereafter? Obviously not. But why? Although the very mind of Christ is ours, we do not always appropriate it by faith or permit the Spirit of God to control our minds and apply them to our daily experience. Furthermore, although the believer possesses a spiritual mind, it is subject to the influence of our old nature, a sinful world, and Satan's forces.

Consequently, Paul gives such admonitions as this one: "Let this mind be in you, which was also in Christ Jesus" (Phil. 2:5 KJV). Why are we told that we should possess a mind that we supposedly already have? The word translated "mind" here is not *nous* (as in 1 Cor. 2:16) but *phroneo,* to be in a certain frame of mind or to have a certain *mind-set.* We are to have the same mental disposition, the same attitude, that Christ had in emptying Himself of His divine prerogatives and submitting to death on the cross.

Paul further stresses the necessity of disciplining our minds in Colossians 3:2: "Set your minds on things above, not on earthly things." Again, he uses the word *phroneo,* the idea being to "practice occupying your minds with the things above" (WILLIAMS), directing your thoughts to dwell upon the spiritual realm. Have you cultivated the habit of holy thinking? We tend to get so immersed in the physical, the finite, and the temporal that we seldom think on the higher realm of the infinite and the eternal.

Let's look at how we should go about acquiring a disciplined mind.

PREPARE THE MIND

How can such discipline of mind be achieved? Certainly not by clenching our fists, gritting our teeth, and saying to ourselves, "I'm going to think holy thoughts today. I'm *going to;* I'm *going to.*" Peter, who in the early years of his discipleship usually spoke first and thought later, offers this as a preliminary step: "Gird up the loins of your mind; be sober" (1 Peter 1:13 KJV). The word for "mind" here is *dianoia*, meaning "mode of thinking" or "disposition of mind."

"Girding up the loins" reminds us of the Israelites who ate the Passover with their loose outer robes gathered up about their waist and secured with a girdle or belt. They were ready to travel at a moment's notice. Runners, wrestlers and warriors all girded themselves for two reasons: to prevent their loose, flowing garments from impeding action, and to brace up their bodies with strength, two tasks of preparation that require self-discipline. Peter's expression means, "Get ready to accomplish something strenuous and demanding with your minds." Implicit here is the idea of disencumbering our minds, freeing them of whatever might distract and hinder. "Tighten up your belt about your minds, keep perfectly calm" (WILLIAMS). We do this in much the same way that we tighten the belt around our waist—by pushing back, saying no, and doing without. Instead of wasting hours in front of the television, filling our minds with trivia, we could flip the switch and occupy our minds by reading a good Christian book.

Besides disencumbering our minds, we must positively prepare, or hone, our minds. We must be mentally alert, sharp, and always ready for intense concentration. Studying, memorizing, and meditating upon God's Word will "brace up" the mind. "Let the word of Christ dwell in you richly"; let it be at home in you, Paul urges (Col. 3:16). Try carrying a packet of memory verses with you so when you have to wait—in line at the bank, on the freeway, at the dentist's office—you can occupy your mind with the Word of God. I've often wished I had all the time I've spent waiting in lines—for tickets, for tellers, for tacos! Since my college days, I've tried to carry a packet of Scripture verses or a book in my pocket. And studying or reading has helped me from getting impatient and frustrated!

FOCUS THE MIND

Another step in disciplining the mind involves *fixing* the mind, by a deliberate act of the will, upon God. "Thou wilt keep him in perfect peace, *whose mind is stayed on thee,* because he trusteth in thee" (Isa. 26:3 KJV). Frances Havergal expressed this idea in "Like a River Glorious":

> Stayed upon Jehovah,
> Hearts are fully blest;
> Finding as He promised,
> Perfect peace and rest.

> Hidden in the hollow of His blessed hand,
> Never foe can follow, never traitor stand;
> Not a surge of worry, not a shade of care,
> Not a blast of hurry touch the spirit there.

The undisciplined mind, often full of distress and unresolved doubt, is easily unsettled and disturbed. Paul urged the Thessalonians that they "be not soon *shaken in mind,* or be troubled" (2 Thess. 2:2 KJV). The word translated "shaken" *(saleuo)* is the same word Luke uses to describe the effect of the storm on the house built upon the sand (Luke 6:48). The storm beat vehemently upon two houses, but it could not shake the house founded upon a rock. Phillips paraphrases the verse: "Keep your heads and [don't] be thrown off your balance."

Luke uses the word again in Acts, where he quotes David (Psalm 16): "I have ever *fixed* my eyes upon the Lord; because he is at my right hand I abide *unshaken*" (Acts 2:25 WEYMOUTH). Paul describes the immature, undisciplined believer as being "tossed back and forth by the waves, and blown here and there by every wind of teaching" (Eph. 4:14), but the mature (or maturing), self-disciplined believer should be "firm, incapable of being moved" (1 Cor. 15:58 WILLIAMS).

Having grown up in the rich farm country of northwestern Illinois, I remember hearing about a pig farmer who called his pigs by tapping his shovel on a fence post. Everything went well, until the woodpeckers moved in. Then "Tap, tap, tap" in one corner of the pen brought all the pigs running. Then "Tap, tap, tap," in another corner, and there went all the pigs. It wasn't long before those porky, spotted pigs ran off all their valuable weight. Isn't this the way it is with believers who have undisciplined minds, running helter-skelter after every new, "exciting" teaching? And they never seem to get settled in their minds so they can abound in the Lord's work.

"We may choose something like a star/To stay our minds on and be staid," Robert Frost wrote. The believer must choose the Bright and Morning Star. And as we stay our minds on Him, we experience the peace of God. This peace "which transcends human understanding, will [in turn] keep constant guard over your hearts and minds as they rest in Christ Jesus" (Phil. 4:7 PHILLIPS). The more we fix our minds on God, the more peace we receive to guard our minds so they can fix ever more intently upon God and produce even greater peace.

THE PEACE OF GOD GUARDS OUR MINDS

What a striking metaphor this is: the peace of God is a sentinel standing constant watch over the renovated palace of our mind. No longer can that "hideous throng" of "evil things" enter at will. When ugly thoughts approach, the sentinel cries, "Halt, in the name of the Monarch who controls this citadel! What are your credentials? What is the password?" And the thought, attitude, and the mind-set without proper credentials and password is denied admission.

Does this sound like a silly fairy tale? It may, but if such a screening process is not going on in your mind, you have not learned the scriptural truth of divine thought control. Paul writes: "We refute arguments and theories and reasonings and every proud and lofty thing that sets itself up against the (true) knowledge of God; and we lead every thought and purpose away captive into the obedience of Christ'' (2 Cor. 10:5 AMPLIFIED). Every thought is compelled to come under the authority of Christ; every mental perception is led into subjection to Christ. Certainly this refers to the false arguments of people we encounter, but also to our own thoughts.

Solomon teaches that discipline of the mind involves both a negative and a positive element. "Never lose sight of [my words], but *fix* them in your mind. . . . *Guard* above all things, *guard your inner self* [Hebrew word for *mind*], for so you live and prosper; *bar out* all talk of evil, and *banish* wayward words'' (Prov. 4:23–24 MOFFATT). The sentinel bars out and banishes from the palace all evil and frivolous thoughts. But it is also necessary to retain, entertain, and actively stimulate and recruit good thoughts. In fact, as someone has said, the best way to "don't" is to "do" so much you don't have time to "don't." In other words, if the palace is filled with the stimulation and enthusiasm of virtuous, noble thoughts, there will be no room or welcome for degrading ones.

NEW THOUGHT PATTERNS MUST BE FORMED

It's not enough for the sentinel merely to turn evil thoughts away from the citadel, for us merely to *suppress* negative thoughts. A positive alternative must take its place; a new thought pattern must be formed. Suppose I were on the university campus and I saw a beautiful co-ed walking across the mall. The natural impulse would be to indulge a lustful thought. But the divine sentinel says, "No, you cannot enter because you are not pleasing to the Monarch." So what happens to the thought—and others like it? If it is merely suppressed it will return again and again, seeking admittance. It will eventually find its way into the palace by way of that mysterious underground dungeon, the subconscious mind.

A positive alternative to suppression might go something like this: "Lord, I thank you for feminine beauty and for my normal response to it. Thank you most of all for the lovely wife you gave me. She's really something—great lover, superb cook, wonderful mother to our children. Bless her right now and give her a good day. Help me to be a good, faithful husband.'' Then I could pick up some flowers on the way home to let her know how much I appreciate her. What was potentially an ugly thought is transformed by God's grace into an occasion of beauty. In such situations, the Holy Spirit will call to our minds suitable passages of Scripture that will be effective in establishing a positive pattern of thought.

The first look is not sin; the second look that leads to lust is. As Martin Luther said, ''You can't keep birds from flying over your head, but you can keep them from building nests in your hair.'' We can't keep those hideous forms from congregating at the door of the palace, but we can keep them from entering the throne room. And we can take those thoughts captive and transform them into thoughts of beauty and glory to God.

WHAT TO THINK ABOUT

What credentials does the sentinel demand of thoughts seeking entrance, what password, what ''open sesame''? Paul gives us a list of eight in Philippians 4:8, an index of what the disciplined mind thinks *about*. ''Whatever is *true* [reliable], whatever is *noble* [honorable, valuable, worthy of reverence, respect-compelling, dignified], whatever is *right* [equitable, fair], whatever is *pure* [stainless, noncontaminating, fit to be brought into the presence of God], whatever is *lovely* [lovable, amiable, endearing, that which calls forth love], whatever is *admirable* [gracious, winsome, attractive, kindly, commendable, laudable, reputable]—if anything is *excellent* [lofty, virtuous] or *praiseworthy* [commendatory, honorable]—think about such things.''

How does such a process work? Think about *truth?* Sure. Sounds good. But how can I get hold of that? What's truth?

When I realized that the written Word and Christ, the living Word, constitute and illustrate each of these eight virtues, my thinking toward this verse was revolutionized. For example, God's Word is *truth* (John 17:17) and Jesus is "the way—and the truth and the life" (John 14:6), and so on through all eight virtues. I have difficulty thinking about truth in the abstract, but truth personified—in Christ—that's something else! I have trouble thinking about purity in the abstract, but here's something concrete—"the commandments of the Lord are *pure,* enlightening the eyes" (Ps. 19:8 KJV).

If we continually "commit [our] works unto the Lord, . . . [our] thoughts shall be established" (Prov. 16:3 KJV). When we mentally "acknowledge him in all our ways," He will direct our paths. He has promised to put His laws into our minds (Heb. 8:10), to "engrave them in [our] innermost thoughts" (Heb. 10:16 KNOX)—as part of the palace decor.

One process remains in the on-going self-disciplining of the mind. The palace was totally renovated when Christ became its Monarch, but it requires continual *renewal.* Paul urged the Roman believers to "be transformed [the same word used in the gospels to describe the transfiguration of Christ] by the *renewing of your mind"* (Rom. 12:2)—"let God remold your minds from within" (PHILLIPS). Again Paul refers to our being "mentally and spiritually *remade"* (Eph. 4:23 PHILLIPS). Without this daily, even moment-by-moment, renewal through the filling of the Spirit, we will become weary and we will faint in our minds (Heb. 12:3).

Without constant renewal, we become sluggish, exhausted, maybe discouraged. Then our defenses are down, and evil thoughts catch us unawares. But if Jesus is in control of our minds, our minds will be under control.

May our "spoken words and [our] unspoken thoughts be pleasing" to the Monarch of the palace (Ps. 19:14 LB).

9 / Tiger Burning Bright: The Disciplined Heart

According to a Greek myth, Prometheus stole fire from heaven and gave it to humankind for their benefit. As a result, another legend says, every human carries a flame of emotion in his or her heart. If this inner flame is carefully tended and controlled, it brings its bearer great benefit. But if it is allowed to flicker or to rage out of control, it causes great destruction.

Some people are ashamed of their flame, thinking of it as a form of weakness. Some even wish it gone, and try to stifle it. To the extent that they are successful in quenching its burning, they become cold and less human. People of the opposite extreme make no effort at all to control the flame and even fan it to a fury that sometimes destroys both them and others. A few people recognize the benefits as well as the dangers of the flame. But even these are sometimes powerless to control it, and in an unguarded moment, the flame may suddenly blaze forth to the embarrassment and harm of many.

Have you found yourself in one of these categories? And do you recognize the embers of emotion, the flame of feeling? Our emotions are a gift from God, not from Prometheus, and as such they neither should be downplayed nor overindulged. Who can say which extreme is worse—the ice of no emotion or the fire of uncontrolled emotion? Poet Robert Frost wrote:

107

> Some say the world will end in fire,
> Some say in ice.
> From what I've tasted of desire
> I hold with those who favor fire.

But then he concluded that

> . . . for destruction, ice
> Is also great
> And would suffice.

And so it will. Christian believers, to fulfill the design of our creation, must neither freeze nor burn out of control. Better a little fire that illuminates and warms than a big one that burns.

EMOTIONS: ANIMALS OF THE HEART

Our major emotions have also been described in terms of animals in the heart. "In each human heart," Ambrose Bierce wrote in *The Devil's Dictionary,* "are a tiger, a pig, an ass, and a nightingale." Each of us has a powerful tiger of ferocity; a pig of envy and greed; an ass of cowardice, folly, and fear; and a nightingale, whose beautiful song of love is compensation for sorrow and suffering. And what a snarling, grunting, braying, and twittering they make! There's no expelling the animals completely, although some have been known to substitute a lamb for the pig and a horse for the ass. There's much to admire about the nightingale and the tiger—when they're under control.

The images of flame and ferocity are brought together in this poem by William Blake:

> Tyger, Tyger! burning bright
> In the forests of the night,
> What immortal hand or eye
> Could frame thy fearful symmetry?

He goes on to say:

> Did he smile his work to see?
> Did he who made the Lamb make thee?

Yes, God made us with all our emotional capacities—our tiger as well as our lamb. And only if we are yielded to His control will our tiger burn bright but under control so as not to consume us.

Have you ever thought about the number of vivid expressions used to describe intense emotions? Many refer to them as heat: "hot under the collar," "get steamed," "lose your cool," "flare up," and "fume." Others imply intense pressure and describe its result: "explode," "flip your lid," "blow your stack" (or top, cork, gasket, wig, noggin), and "hit the ceiling." Still others imply ferocity and a total breakdown of control: "fly off the handle," and "hopping mad." Or how about that common description, "He just came all *unglued*"?

In his play *The Great God Brown,* Eugene O'Neill wrote: "Man is born broken. He lives by mending. The grace of God is glue." Certainly it is only by God's grace that we can keep from coming "unglued"—but grace is so much more, and the human condition requires much more than glue!

Even expression of love is often described in terms that suggest lack of control, imbalance, and complete loss of equilibrium: "fall head over heels," "swept off your feet," "lose your head" (or heart), "flip," "far gone on," "smitten" (or struck with), "stuck on," "crazy over," "wild about," and "mad about." And a former love is referred to as: "an old flame."

Ironically it's sometimes the pleasant emotion that makes us lose control. Poet Emily Dickinson expressed the point well:

> I can wade grief,
> Whole pools of it,—
> I'm used to that.
> But the least push of joy
> Breaks up my feet,
> And I tip. . . .

Later in the same poem, she says:

> Power is only pain,
> Stranded, through discipline,
> Till weights will hang.

Reaction to physical, mental, or emotional hurt often will provide a stabilizing power. But the poet is perceptive enough to realize that such is the case only through discipline.

LACK OF SELF-DISCIPLINE IS MOST OBVIOUS
IN OUR EMOTIONS

Our lack of self-discipline seems to show up nowhere so glaringly as in our emotions. For awhile we might be able to keep our undisciplined thoughts to ourselves, but our undisciplined emotions have a way of manifesting themselves to everyone around us. Why? For one reason, our emotions are responses to our relationships.

A second reason is the primacy of emotions in our makeup. We are emotional—some more than others, but all somewhat. And this is so because God made us in His own image. Our ability to feel is grounded in the very nature of His own being. The Scripture describes God as an emotional being. He loves (John 3:16; 2 Cor. 5:14); He grieves (Eph. 4:30; John 11:35); He is capable of anger (Ps. 7:11; Matt. 21:12); He is jealous (Exod. 20:5; 34:14); and so forth. Each of His emotions is positive and healthy. Because of His nature, He is incapable of guilt and fear. (The guilt Jesus experienced while on the cross was caused by our sin; it was not His own.)

If we have been so wonderfully made, why then do we have so many problems with our emotions? Why do we experience negative emotions, and why do even the more positive ones so often get out of control? Why is it that "the heart is the most deceitful of all things, desperately sick" (Jer. 17:9 NEB)? The answer lies in the devastating effects of the Fall in Eden. Before the Fall, apparently only positive emotions, such as love, joy, and delight, existed in humankind and were the natural responses of Adam's and Eve's relationships with Jehovah, each other, and with the animal kingdom. Adam and Eve were perfect master not only of all living creatures but also of all their own faculties.

But note the change in emotions immediately after the Fall. Whereas before, Adam and Eve enjoyed perfect, blissful communion with God, now they felt shame for the first time (Gen. 3:7). Before the sin they were *nude,* but after the sin they were *naked.* Shame brought another new emotion—guilt. And with the guilt came fear, causing them to attempt to hide from God.

Confronted with his sin, Adam experienced another emotion, anger and blame: ''The woman you put here with me—she gave me some fruit from the tree, and I ate it'' (Gen. 3:12). Other emotions came as part of the curse: anguish (for women in childbirth, Gen. 3:16), sorrow for man in toil for survival (Gen. 3:17–19), disappointment and depression over expulsion from the Garden, and, later, grief because of death. Apparently it was their sin, too, that elicited from God such emotions as sorrow, holy anger, righteous jealousy, and hatred (of sin).

In addition to introducing new, negative emotions, the Fall distorted the positive emotions by making them uncontrolled and misplaced. Ever since, humankind has attempted to satisfy God-given emotional needs in ways not pleasing to Him. For example, every person has an inherent need to love and be loved. And God has provided legitimate means to satisfy these needs, as He did when He created Eve from Adam. Emotional problems arise when we seek fulfillment in illegitimate ways—by loving *things*, by *lusting* rather than *loving,* by loving a person ''unsuitable'' or in the wrong way, by loving others more than we love God, etc.

THE SEVEN BASIC EMOTIONS

Some psychologists say there are just three basic emotions— love, fear, and anger. Others say there are four—love, fear, hate, and guilt. Various other emotions are extensions of the basic ones. Worry, anxiety, and often depression, guilt, jealousy, and grief may be forms of fear. Similarly, tenderness, sympathy, compassion, and often joy, happiness, and delight stem from love. Anger, sometimes a manifestation of hate, can, in milder forms, appear as annoyance and irritation.

I have classified emotions in seven major categories, somewhat like the colors of the rainbow. Recalling the colors in the spectrum can help us visualize the gamut of our emotions.

Each of the seven emotions can be positive or negative. To grow toward perfection we must initially and basically have a

RAINBOW OF EMOTIONS

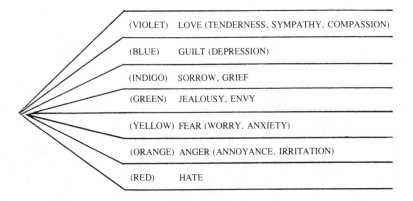

(VIOLET)	LOVE (TENDERNESS, SYMPATHY, COMPASSION)
(BLUE)	GUILT (DEPRESSION)
(INDIGO)	SORROW, GRIEF
(GREEN)	JEALOUSY, ENVY
(YELLOW)	FEAR (WORRY, ANXIETY)
(ORANGE)	ANGER (ANNOYANCE, IRRITATION)
(RED)	HATE

new heart, just as our spirit must be made alive by Christ and our mind must be renovated. The unregenerate heart is perverse and deceitful, defying even understanding (Jer. 17:9), much less disciplining. But God's promise of a heart transplant for Israel is applicable as well for us: "I will take the stony heart out of their flesh, and will give them an heart of flesh" (Ezek. 11:19 KJV). Only this new heart, a heart capable of knowing God (Jer. 24:7) and experiencing emotions in a God-ordained way, is able to be disciplined.

One of the finest, often overlooked, scriptural examples of a disciplined heart is Ezra. This Jewish priest and scribe won the permission of the Babylonian king to return to Jerusalem to rebuild the temple. He led eighteen hundred Jews from Babylon to the Holy City, a nine hundred-mile journey that took four months. His success in rebuilding the temple, opposing compromise with paganism, and reestablishing the old forms of worship attests to his great discipline. What was his secret? Note Ezra 7:10: "Ezra had prepared his heart to study the law of the Lord, and to do it, and to teach its statutes and ordinances in Israel." To study, to practice, and to teach God's truth—that's a self-disciplined life!

Ezra, whose name means "help," has always been a real help to me in my efforts at self-discipline. Though you and I will probably never be called upon to lead eighteen hundred people on a nine hundred-mile journey to rebuild a temple, we can realize the same kind of self-discipline in our homes, communities, and places of employment.

SIX FACTORS IN EMOTIONAL SELF-DISCIPLINE

But what is involved in the disciplining of the heart? What makes some emotions negative and others positive, and even the same emotion positive at one time but negative at another? There are at least six factors to consider in analyzing our emotions and determining the extent to which they are disciplined.

First, what is the nature, the essence, of the emotion itself and its relation to other emotions? This question leads naturally to other considerations, such as the emotion's motive or purpose, its object, its occasion or time, its degree or extent, and how one responds to emotional stimuli. In other words, we can ask the questions: What? Why? Who? When? How much? and How?

THE NATURE OF THE EMOTION

Would you believe me if I were to tell you that if you don't hate, you are probably lacking in emotional discipline? Well, don't believe me simply because I tell you, but consider the point in relation to God's Word. The Scripture clearly indicates that we can't love where we ought to love if we don't hate where we ought to hate. For example, the psalmist makes it clear that our love for God and good should produce hatred of all that militates against them. "Those who love the Lord hate evil" (97:10). Genuine love produces hatred of its opposite. To love truth is to hate falsehood. To love purity is to hate impurity. To love justice is to hate injustice.

The extent of our hatred of evil should be determined by the extent of our love of good. Isn't it logical, for instance, that because I love my wife and family I will despise those things that would bring them harm? If I didn't, wouldn't you wonder about my love? It's the same with our love for God. If we truly love Him, that love will evoke hatred of whatever comes between God and us. "Hate evil, love good," God commanded Israel (Amos 5:15). But so often we, like them, "hate good and love evil" (Mic. 3:2)—a sure sign of an undisciplined heart.

Solomon links righteous hatred with another emotion—fear or awe of God. "To fear the Lord is to hate evil; I hate pride, arrogance, evil behavior, and perverse speech" (Prov. 8:13). A disciplined heart does not feel terror toward the heavenly Father. "There is no fear in love. But perfect love drives fear. . . . The man who fears is not made perfect in love" (1 John 4:18).

On a physiological level, fear alerts us to danger. It stimulates the flow of adrenalin which helps us overcome or escape difficulty or danger. But such a natural, legitimate fear should not turn into a cowardly paranoia which imagines danger behind every bush. Sam Fathers, a wise old man in William Faulkner's story "The Bear," tells young Ike McCaslin, "Be scared. You can't help that. But don't be afraid."

Justifiable hatred is that prompted by love and godly fear. All other kinds are displeasing to God and must be removed by His Spirit. Similarly, our fear of God, a reverential awe, is grounded in love and manifested in hatred of evil. "God has not given us the spirit of fear but one to inspire strength, love, and self-discipline" (2 Tim. 1:7 TCNT).

In the same manner, disciplined love is the kind that is genuine, sincere, without hypocrisy (Rom. 12:9). Today love has several definitions. There's love and then there's "luv," the latter being saccharine and superficial. "Oh I luv you, dear brother Key-ho," an acquaintance glibly says to me. But he doesn't *know* me, nor has he even taken the trouble to learn my name even after numerous corrections.

Genuine love also motivates us for good. It is patient, kind, not proud, not rude or self-seeking, not easily angered, keeps no score of wrongs, delights in truth, practices, hopes, trusts, and perseveres (1 Cor. 13:4–7).

Even the sorrow of believers should be a hopeful sorrow. Paul urged believers not to grieve as do others who have no hope (1 Thess. 4:13). Similarly, guilt is positive if it serves its purpose of bringing us to repentance, but once the sin is forgiven and put under the blood of Christ, we must also forgive ourselves, forget the past, and press on to win the prize for God (Phil. 3:13–14). A morbid grief or guilt can rob us of our joy and hinder our service for Christ.

Jealousy and anger may seem to be totally negative emotions and therefore to be avoided. But just as God is "jealous," in that He demands exclusive allegiance, and is righteously indignant over sin, so we are to reflect these holy emotions. Paul wrote the Corinthians, "I am jealous for you with a godly jealousy" (2 Cor. 11:2). "My jealousy over you is the right sort of jealousy, for in my eyes you are like a fresh, unspoiled girl whom I am presenting as fiancée to your true husband, Christ himself" (PHILLIPS).

In another sense, just as "He jealously desires the spirit which He has made to dwell in us" (James 4:5 NASB), or just as the Spirit that dwells in us jealously desires us, so we should jealously desire the Spirit and His control over us.

Just as there is a holy jealousy, so there is a sinless anger. "Be angry and yet do not sin," Paul urges (Eph. 4:26 NASB). The apostle warns that if we are angry, we must be sure it is the kind of anger that is not sinful. We all need to learn how to be *good* and angry! So often we label as "holy indignation" what is in fact a carnal "flying off the handle."

What *is* sinless anger? It is an anger prompted by love of God and good, along with hatred of evil. Jesus manifested such an anger when He drove the moneychangers from the temple.

Two responses to the same condition—one impulsive and carnal, the other restrained and spiritual—illustrate these two kinds of anger. A year or so ago, one of the major television networks ran a film that was offensive to Christians in its explicit sensuality and its profanity. One believer made a big stir locally by wrecking his television set with a sledge-hammer and then writing a nasty anonymous letter to the local station. Another believer, equally as disturbed by the offensive film, enlisted the help of fellow believers and called the network and the local affiliate to object courteously and graciously. Which response do you suppose achieved the greater good?

MOTIVE OF THE EMOTION

Closely related to the kind of emotion is its motivation. For example, *why* do we get angry? Isn't it usually because *our* rights are violated, *our* dignity threatened, or *our* purposes frustrated? And are not these also the primary sources of our hate and fear? But with Jesus it was never so. He expressed anger at the moneychangers not because *His own* rights, dignity, or purposes were violated but because His Father's house was being desecrated (John 2:16).

Not only by His example but also by His explicit teaching did Jesus illustrate justifiable anger. In the Sermon on the Mount, Jesus said, "I say unto you that whosoever is angry with his brother *without a cause* shall be in danger of judgment" (Matt. 5:22). The implicit principle is twofold: gratuitous anger is always wrong, and anger with a just cause—violation of good by evil—is justifiable. We just need to be sure it's *God's* cause and not our own!

I once tried to keep a record of everything in the course of a week that caused me to be angry or upset. Try it sometime. You'll probably discover, as I did, that in nearly every case the cause of anger was a real or imagined threat to my own ego.

Even such highly positive emotions as love and grief can be wrongly motivated. Sometimes, perhaps often, we love selfishly, seeking only what will profit us. Even seemingly generous acts of charity may be motivated simply by a desire to achieve public acclaim or simply to make us feel good. And certainly a large part of grief is basically selfish. We may feel deprived and almost resentful that the absence of the loved one will disrupt our pleasant routine.

THE OBJECT OF THE EMOTION

Of major importance in disciplining our emotions is their object, especially in the case of hate, love, and fear. The undisciplined heart hates, loves, and fears things and people variously and indiscriminately.

The Scriptures teach that those who truly love God will hate the things *He* hates. Solomon lists seven things God hates (and implies more): "Haughtiness; Lying; Murdering; Plotting evil; Eagerness to do wrong; A false witness; Sowing discord among brothers" (Prov. 6:16–19 LB). Note that the object of justifiable hatred is things and actions, not persons.

Like our heavenly Father, we should hate the sin but love the sinner. Jesus made this point clear in the Sermon on the Mount: "Ye have heard that it hath been said, Thou shalt love thy neighbor, and hate thine enemy. But I say unto you . . . do good to them that hate you, and pray for them which despitefully use you, and persecute you" (Matt. 5:43–44 KJV).

If our love of good evokes justifiable hatred of evil, others' hatred of good should evoke love for the evildoer. This is a hard lesson to *learn*—and even a harder one to *live*.

I recall learning one of my first lessons in not hating people and in returning good for evil. A boy of six, I had just come home after a rough day in first grade. The dialogue went something like this.

"That Fats McGinty and Nasty Roche are always making fun of me and picking on me. Today they made me eat frog eggs they found in the crick. I hate their guts!"

My mom responded, "No, son, we mustn't hate anybody. Now you be nice to them even though they aren't nice to you."

"Yeah, mom, I know, but have you ever tasted frog eggs?"

I've had to relearn and be reminded many times since then that such a reaction as my mom advised runs counter to my natural inclination, and therefore demands great spiritual self-discipline. And have you noticed that there's *always* a Fats McGinty or a Nasty Roche around? When we can't remove the stimulus, we must learn to control the emotional response.

If the disciplined heart hates only things and actions, not *people,* it loves only people and not things or actions. We are told explicitly to ''love not the world, neither the things that are in the world.'' Those ''things'' may be slightly different for each person, but basically they can be divided into ''lust of the flesh, and the lust of the eyes, and the pride of life'' (1 John 2:15–16 KJV).

For some, money and material things are the object of love. Remember what Paul told Timothy: ''The *love* of money is the root of all evil'' (1 Tim. 6:10 KJV)—and we don't have to *have* it to *love* it. For others, the love object may be an unbeliever or, if married, someone other than the spouse. The disciplined heart never makes such provision for the flesh. Rather it makes us ''Flee also youthful lusts'' (2 Tim. 2:22 KJV). ''If you don't want to eat the devil's apples,'' someone has well said, ''stay out of his orchard.'' And that requires emotional discipline, especially in apple season when the fruit is ripe and red and juicy.

Of no less importance than hate and love objects are fear objects. We naturally and legitimately fear that which endangers us, but sometimes, like small children, we experience an almost neurotic feeling of generalized anxiety called *angst,* the object of which we cannot identify. How *many* of the things we fear and worry about end up being imaginary ills that never transpire? In the disciplined heart, mature love casts out such fears (1 John 4:18) and replaces them with faith.

Have you ever noticed that it's hard to be afraid and love at the same time, to be afraid and trust at the same time? Of course, it becomes harder as our love and trust deepen and mature. Occasionally my youngest son, Kenyon, has terrifying nightmares and then can't get back to sleep. Our late-night discussions usually begin with the object of his fear. One went something like this:

''What was the dream about?''

''Well, I can't remember much of it. But there were scary monsters in it.''

''I know they *seemed* real, but you know they weren't, right?''

''Yeah, I guess. But I can't get em out of my head.''

"Well, try getting something *else* there instead. You know I love you, right?"

"Sure, dad."

"And do you love me?"

"Sure, dad. You know that."

"And because we love each other, we trust each other, right?"

"Yeah."

"You know mom and I are just down the hall and that we won't let anything hurt you. And you know, too, that God is our heavenly Father, and He's right here with you. He promised *never* to leave us. And remember our talking about guardian angels! Those monsters aren't real, but God and His angels are. Right? Son? Son?"

Kenyon was sound asleep—with a peaceful little grin on his face.

Our heavenly Father has given us similar instruction about what we fear. "The Lord is my light and my salvation—whom shall I fear?" David asked. "The Lord is the stronghold of my life—of whom shall I be afraid?" (Ps. 27:1). We should fear no one but God, and that in the sense of reverential awe and respect. Jesus told us clearly whom we should and shouldn't fear. "Do not be afraid of those who kill the body but cannot kill the soul. Rather, be afraid of the one who can destroy both soul and body in hell" (Matt. 10:28). The reference here is not to Satan, as some have supposed, but to God. Nowhere in Scripture are we told to *fear* Satan—only to resist him (James 4:7).

If we have the reverential awe due to God and if we love Him with a genuine, mature love, those common fear objects will no longer be a threat. We'll not fear ten thousands of people who oppose us (Ps. 3:6), or the army that fights against us (Ps. 27:3), or what an enemy can do to us (Ps. 56:11), or a person's reproach (Isa. 51:7). We'll not even fear natural calamities, so-called "acts of God." "Therefore we will not fear, though the earth give way and the mountains fall into the heart of the sea" (Ps. 46:2).

Do you have a problem controlling fear? Try reading and

meditating upon Psalm 91, especially verses 5 and 6: "You will not fear the terror of night, nor the arrow that flies by day, nor the pestilence that stalks in the darkness, nor the plague that destroys at midday."

When I was a teenager my mother, even though she was a believer, feared and worried when my brothers and I rode motorcycles. Then there came a definite time when she stopped worrying. She told us that she was convicted that such fears were sin, that when she was *worrying,* she wasn't *trusting.* She cast all her cares upon God (1 Peter 5:7) and He removed the worry. What a testimony it was some years later to see her fearlessly face her own death from cancer, firmly fixing her trust in the Lord.

The believer with a disciplined heart "will have no fear of bad news; his heart is steadfast, trusting in the Lord" (Ps. 112:7).

OCCASION OF THE EMOTION

The disciplined heart subjects emotions to yet another criterion—that of occasion or time. The Scripture teaches that even emotions which may be positive in themselves can, if expressed at the wrong time and place, be negative. In Ecclesiastes, Solomon lists twenty-eight items for which there is a season, a right time and a wrong time (chapter 3). At least a dozen of these are emotions or directly related to emotions.

He says there's "A time to weep and a time to laugh, a time to mourn and a time to dance" (v. 4). Both grief and guilt can be the cause of weeping. I know a woman who has never ceased grieving for her husband, who died fifteen years ago. She still makes daily visits to his grave. Also damaging is guilt that continues long after God has forgiven the sin. Uncle John, a character in John Steinbeck's *The Grapes of Wrath,* indulges his guilt with a compulsion to confess to everyone. "I done things I never tol' about," he says. Ma Joad gives him this advice: "Tell em to God. Don't go burdenen' other people with your sins. . . . Go down the river an' stick your head under an' whisper em in the stream."

A mark of the disciplined heart is its ability to share in the emotions of others, to empathize (literally "feel in" or project ourselves into the feelings of others). Can you truly rejoice over the blessings and accomplishments of others—without faking it? Do you truly feel sadness and compassion when a brother or sister is hurting? We are commanded to "rejoice with those who rejoice; and mourn with those who mourn" (Rom. 12:15), but the undisciplined heart secretly rejoices at another's adversity and feels jealous or sad when another prospers.

Perhaps lack of emotional discipline shows up no more glaringly than in the insensitivity of untimely, out-of-place emotions. We've all known (and possibly have *been*) clowns who laugh or try to evoke laughter at the *wrong* time.

In his poem "Home Burial," Robert Frost describes a couple in Vermont who, having buried their only child in a family plot behind the house, struggle to understand the opposite ways the other handles grief. The wife thinks her husband is callous because of the timing of his comments.

> I can repeat the very words you were saying.
> 'Three foggy mornings and one rainy day
> Will rot the best birch fence a man can build.'
> Think of it, talk like that *at such a time!*

The disciplined heart is sensitive to the feelings of others and expresses emotions in a timely, tactful way.

Ecclesiastes 3 also suggests that there is an appropriate time for expressing love: "a time to embrace and a time to refrain" (v. 5). Showing affection is desirable, but especially young couples must remember that there is a suitable time, just as there's a suitable time for hate and anger: "a time to hate, a time for war" (v. 8). Even righteous hatred of evil and holy anger at its results can become evil if they overstay their time. The Almighty sets the pattern: "He will not always chide; neither will he keep his anger forever" (Ps. 103:9 KJV).

THE EXTENT OF THE EMOTION

Closely related to timeliness is the extent of an emotion. For example, feeling no fear at all in the face of real danger is foolhardy, but feeling excessive fear is cowardly. Similarly, even a righteous anger, if excessive, may pass easily into sin. Certainly he is a fool who *cannot* be angry, but he is a wise and disciplined person who *will not* be excessively angry.

But how much emotion is too much? Certainly we can never love God too much—no, nor people either. Christ's teaching that we cannot be His disciples if we do not hate father, mother, wife, children, brothers, and sisters (Luke 14:26) emphasizes comparative emotions. That is, Jesus does not want us to love our families *less* but rather to love Him *more,* so that by comparison, the former actually seems like hatred.

Again, a basic principle emerges. The extent of any emotion should be determined, at least in part, by its stimulus or object. For example, some local believers recently became incensed at an appearance of the atheist Madalyn Murray O'Hair. Their anger was more intense than in the past over such issues as the blatant peddling of pornography or over the disruptive sowing of discord among brethren. Christ's words about straining at a gnat and swallowing a camel seem pertinent here.

Because of His absolute glory, we can never love God too much; and because of its utter degradation, we can never hate sin too much. But other emotions are often excessive. For example, we can be overburdened with guilt, overwhelmed with grief, and overwrought with fear and anxiety.

Of course we do not usually intellectualize our emotions as this all may suggest. We do not consciously reason, "Now the stimulus does not warrant any greater anger on my part than a 2.5 on a scale of one to ten." Any such reasoning, if it comes at all, comes *after* the fact, or the explosion, after the emotion has been expressed. "I really blew my cool on that one. I sure got carried away. Lord, help me not to lose control that way again." This is one of the reasons that emotions are so difficult to control: if the stimulus comes, can the response be far behind? Therefore, previous conditioning for spiritual responses must be wrought by the Holy Spirit. This brings us to the final criterion.

RESPONSE TO EMOTIONAL STIMULI

Ultimately any concern with emotional discipline comes down to the basic question, "How should I respond to emotional stimuli?" Emotional self-discipline is largely a matter of right reactions. Not only negative emotions but also positive ones are reactions, often to other emotions. For example, our love for God is a reaction to His love for us: "We love him because he first loved us" (1 John 4:19 KJV).

Many Christians would say they have fairly good control over their *actions*. They attend church regularly, maybe serve on a board, teach a class, maybe have an active devotional life. They would probably say they don't lie or cheat or steal or commit murder or adultery. But what about our *reactions?*

How would you react emotionally to such stimuli as these: a neighbor who flips cigarette butts into your yard; a fellow worker who delights in baiting you and belittling your faith; a "friend" who spreads unfounded, malicious stories about you? The list could go on forever. But whatever the emotional stimulus, do you respond *in kind?* Do you return the same kind of emotion—anger for anger, antagonism for antagonism, surliness for surliness? Or, to use Paul's words, do you "repay . . . evil for evil" (Rom. 12:17)? If so, you are controlled by that emotion; you are overcome by evil.

I have a theory that the emotional tone of a roomful of people can be altered by the most predominant mood of any one person in the room. All too often we are like chameleons, changing emotional color to fit the mood of those around us. For example, in a business meeting or in a church board meeting angry words evoke angry reactions, which further perpetuate the angry mood. There is a scriptural truth that says: "A gentle answer turns away wrath, but a harsh word stirs up anger" (Prov. 15:1).

Have you ever had the experience of getting up in the morning feeling exuberant and enthusiastic about the day's activities— only to feel your mood changing when the children are grumpy and your spouse is a little depressed or the weather is dreary? In such cases, disciplined hearts will not react in kind. They will not be controlled, but will react with opposite emotions, setting a new emotional tone.

SEVEN WAYS TO RESPOND TO EMOTIONAL STIMULI

There are at least seven possible responses to emotional stimuli. The self-disciplined heart chooses the most suitable.

Acquiesce/Express

Perhaps the easiest, most natural response is simply to acquiesce to the stimulus and express unrestrained emotion. Doing otherwise, the rationale goes, is to harm the psyche, squelch spontaneity, and give us nasty "hang-ups."

But letting it all hang out is one thing; expressing an emotion suitably is another. Disciplined expression of an emotion is typified by at least five characteristics. First, the emotion is expressed *spiritually,* not carnally and selfishly—thus assuring the proper nature and motive. "Lead the life of the Spirit," Paul says, for "then you will never satisfy the passions of the flesh" but will, by implication, fulfill the emotional needs of the higher nature (Gal. 5:16 MOFFATT).

Second, the disciplined emotion is expressed *deliberately,* not rashly—thus assuring the suitability of time and occasion. Deliberate emotional expression gets the mind involved, tempering feeling with thought. It is typified by a calm, "sweet reasonableness" (as Luther translated Phil. 4:5). Henry David Thoreau wrote often of such deliberate living. In *Walden* he said: "Let us spend one day as deliberately as nature, and not be thrown off the track by every nutshell and mosquito's wing that falls on the rails. Let us rise early and fast, or break fast, gently and without perturbation; let company come and company go, let the bells ring and the children cry—determined to make a day of it. Why should we knock under and go with the stream?"

To assure suitable objects, disciplined emotions will be expressed *discriminately,* not randomly. For example, we will be able to hate sin but at the same time love the sinner. We have probably all heard this idea expressed so often that it has become trite. But it's a significant principle nevertheless—and one we can practice only with God's help. When a friend of mine left his wife and children to become involved with another friend's wife, it was hard for me to separate the sin from the sinner. But God has helped me to keep on showing Christian love to the friend while at the same time detesting his actions.

Fourth, emotions must be expressed *positively*—thereby reinforcing the positive nature of the God-given emotion. Even positive emotions can be expressed negatively, creating a detrimental effect. For example, sincere, well-meaning believers, motivated by legitimate hatred of evil, should not express legitimate anger negatively. An acquaintance of mine loves to tell how he took a baseball bat and demolished the family television set because "it's nothin but a filthy boob tube." And I know of a Christian father who raged at a teacher and, because of objections, ripped up a novel that had been assigned for his daughter to read, but which he himself had not investigated.

Finally, disciplined emotions are expressed *restrainedly,* assuring the suitable degree or extent of the emotion. Too much, even of a good thing, can be damaging. Neither the man who demolished the television nor the father who tore up the novel showed restraint.

Repress

Another way of responding to emotional stimuli is to repress the emotion. Repression forces the emotion into the subconscious and pushes it down every time it surfaces to the level of consciousness. Scarlett O'Hara in *Gone With the Wind* represses unpleasant emotional reality by saying, "I'll think about that tomorrow." With us it may go something like this: "That really burns me, but I'm not going to dwell on it *now.*" Repression only puts an emotion on "hold." It does not deal with it positively. And usually it later surfaces, larger and stronger, when we least expect it.

Suppress

Many people confuse *repression* and *suppression*. They differ in that suppression involves a conscious dismissal or expulsion of an emotion or thought *from* the heart and mind rather than a mere forcing of them into the subconscious. Consequently, suppression is a much more desirable option. "That really burns me, but I'm going to put it out of my mind and *forget* it."

That sounds very good, but the problem is that something is missing. We simply cannot by resolution and strength of our will successfully expel emotions. They have a way of *not going* or, if they do, a persistent way of coming back again and again.

Several years ago, a disagreement between a fellow believer and myself grew into a real conflict. I felt that his words and actions had been unfair and unchristian. I tried to put the matter out of my mind, but it kept coming back. As time passed, it began to rankle. It festered and became inflamed. That's what repressed resentment and anger always do. Finally, I asked God to forgive *me* and to remove the resentment. He did so—but only after I had written my Christian brother and asked *his* forgiveness. Then I had peace and a renewed love for my friend.

Assess and Address

The missing element is the need to assess the emotion, to examine its cause, its essence, its object. In this process, it is beneficial, at least for me, to address myself and God too. "It really *burns* me, Lord, when a driver is so inconsiderate and reckless as that. He tailgated, then passed and cut in so sharply he almost ran me off the road. And then gave me an obscene gesture. As if I had done something wrong! I was traveling at exactly the speed limit. Oh well, it's silly to get upset over that and let him set my mood. Maybe he's late for an appointment. Or the poor guy may have a problem that's bugging him. Maybe a fight with his wife. It's a cinch he's not going to be around long if he keeps driving like that! Probably doesn't know you, Lord. I bet a lot of the nastiness like that is due to people's insecurity and problems. Lord, help that guy come to know You as his Savior before he kills himself. And thanks for helping me not lose my cool."

By first *assessing* the stimulus and potential emotion and *addressing* ourselves and God, saying exactly how we feel about the stimulus, we can achieve the ability to carry out the next possible response.

Possess

We "possess" or control the emotion when we ourselves are possessed by the Spirit of God. The Scripture teaches that the disciplined heart has a high tolerance level. "Let everyone be quick to listen, slow to talk, *slow to get angry*; for man's anger does not promote God's righteousness" (James 1:19–20 MLB). According to Solomon, the emotionally self-possessed person is greater than a mighty conqueror: "Better is he who is slow to anger than the mighty hero" (Prov. 16:32 MLB). Such emotional domination involves expelling negative feelings from the heart as well as compensating for them.

Harness

To harness an emotion is to control it for useful ends. The harnessing of an emotion can take several forms. As illustrated in the self-dialogue above, potential anger can be transformed into the positive emotion of compassion.

An incident in the life of Jesus illustrates the possessing and harnessing of emotion. When the critical, hypocritical religious leaders scrutinized Jesus to see if He would heal a man on the Sabbath, we see three different emotions fusing one into another. "When he had looked round about on them with anger, being grieved for the hardness of their hearts, he saith unto the man, Stretch forth thine hand. And he stretched it out: and his hand was restored as the other" (Mark 3:5 KJV). An *angry* glance becomes *grief* or *deep distress* over their callousness, and this in turn is expressed in *compassion* for the man with a paralyzed hand. Ironically, according to Luke's account, the critics were the ones who lost emotional control: "They were *furious*" (6:11). Can you imagine how most of us would have reacted to such a provocation? But Jesus dominated the anger, transformed it into grief and expressed both love and compassion.

A second way of harnessing emotions is compensating and finding release in another, more positive and acceptable way. For example, one way to handle frustration and anger is to take it out on a punching bag, to play a vigorous game of handball, or to jog a few miles. A way to alleviate grief or depression is to set about doing something that will benefit others as well as yourself—make a cake, mow the lawn, or take the kids to the zoo.

Think right now of someone who bugs you, someone you really can't stand. First remind yourself that Jesus *died* for that person. Now try to think of some way you can show him or her kindness. It might be just a little thing—a sincere compliment such as, "You look so nice today." Or "Say, you did a good job on that report." Allow the potential antagonism, annoyance, anger to be transformed, by grace, into love. You may be rebuffed, but remember, the best way to control the flame of anger is to heap coals of fire.

There remains one way of dealing with emotions that has virtually been neglected in discussions on the subject.

Prepossess

To "prepossess" is to preoccupy our minds with good thoughts. Probably many of our emotional battles are virtually lost before they begin because we have established predispositions to react wrongly. Many Christians seem to have a simplistic notion of emotional provocation, which goes something like this: Satan flits to our side and, when an emotional stimulus occurs, whispers, "Go ahead and indulge your emotions." And we do or don't, depending upon some tenuous mood of the moment. But the truth of the matter is that we do not stumble in an instant or lose emotional control in a moment. The predisposition to react a certain way has been forming, building, germinating for some time.

Paul urges us to "clothe yourself with the Lord Jesus Christ" and to "not make provision for the flesh to gratify its cravings" (Rom. 13:14). In other words, we must *prepossess* our emotions, seize and occupy them *before* the stimuli appear.

The tragic results of failure to prepossess emotions are illustrated in the Scripture. It seems certain, for example, that David had fallen long before that evening when he walked upon the rooftop of the palace and saw Bathsheba bathing. His fall was seeded when he "tarried still at Jerusalem" "at the time when kings go forth to battle," and maybe even before that (2 Sam. 11). Why did he tarry and walk restively upon the rooftop? Certainly this "man after God's own heart" did not consciously plot to commit adultery and murder. But when the stimulus presented itself, powerful predispositions surfaced, and the great man lost emotional control.

Similarly, the fall of Samson very likely began even prior to the time when he "went down to Timnah, and saw there a young Philistine woman" (Judg. 14:1). Before he "went down," there apparently "went down" into him very powerful emotional predispositions that led ultimately to his defeat. In like manner, the tragedy of Lot and his family probably began even before he "pitched his tents near Sodom," even before he indulged his envy and love of material things when he "looked up and saw that the whole plain of Jordan was well watered" (Gen. 13:10, 12). You and I, by what we see and hear and read and do *today,* are establishing emotional predispositions that will influence, positively or negatively, our responses to future emotional stimuli.

We can prepossess our emotions only if we are possessed by the Word of God and the Spirit of God. For only then will our hearts be *established* (James 5:8). Note the verb tenses in David's words: "He *will not fear* evil tidings; his heart *is* steadfast, trusting in the Lord. His heart *is* upheld; he *will not fear*" (Ps. 112:7–8). Because the believer's heart is established (present), he will not fear (future)—a beautiful example of emotional prepossessing.

"It is a good thing that the heart be established with grace," the writer of Hebrews says (13:9 KJV). God has made provision to "stablish [your] hearts unblameable in holiness before God" (1 Thess. 3:13 KJV). How? Through the most powerful of all emotions. Note the preceding verse of the chapter: "The Lord make you to increase and abound in love one toward another and toward all men." Love is such a powerful emotion that it will cover a multitude of sins (James 5:20).

EMOTIONAL SELF-DISCIPLINE BEGINS WITH LOVE

Here, then, is a logical and scriptural place to begin the disciplining of our emotions—with the motivating force of love. Note how it works. Because God first loved us, we love Him (1 John 4:19). If we truly love God, we will love other people (1 John 4:7–8). And to the degree that our love matures, it will expel fear (1 John 4:18), as well as depression, jealousy, anger, and hatred.

Jesus warned that in the last days "the love of most will grow cold" (Matt. 24:12). Doesn't that sound like a description of our own day? Even many Christians, like the believers at Ephesus, have left their first love (Rev. 2:4). Is it any wonder, then, that "men's hearts fail them for fear" (Luke 21:26 KJV)? Is it surprising that the breakdown of emotional discipline is so wide-spread?

We cannot reverse a world-wide cooling of the heat of love any more than we can control the world-wide flaming of passion. We cannot melt the glacier or extinguish the conflagration. But we *can* have our own flame of love stoked by the God of love and, through His power, control our flame of feeling.

10 / A House, a Bear, or Beast of Burden? The Disciplined Body

Remember Stuart Hamblin's song from the 1950s—"This Ole House"? How are things at *your* house (that is, your body)? In disrepair and disorder? Or orderly and smoothly functioning?

The comparison of the body to a house is certainly scriptural. The apostle Paul speaks of our being in an "earthly tent" while earnestly longing for a heavenly house not made with hands (2 Cor. 5:1–2). And Solomon used the image of a house to describe the process of our bodies growing old (Eccl. 12:3–7).

It's unfortunate, though, that so many Christians seem to think they have no time to care for this earthly house. Or, because spiritual matters are of prime importance, they seem to have no sense of responsibility to keep the house in order. The ancient Greeks had as their motto: A sound mind in a sound body. For Christian believers a suitable motto would be: A Spirit-controlled spirit, a Jesus mind, and a godly heart in a well-disciplined body.

THREE VIEWS OF THE BODY

Do you realize that our attitudes toward our bodies are of real significance in our Christian experience and particularly in self-discipline? How do you regard *your* body? As a mere collection of minerals worth about $7.28 (up 643 percent from the ninety-eight cent estimate of a decade ago)?

Someone may say, "Hey, if you saw *my* body, you wouldn't have to ask! It's something else!"

"Oh, you mean it's worthy of admiration and even adoration?"

"No, I mean it's disgusting!"

Someone else may say, "How do I regard my bod? As little as possible. I surely don't *adore* it, but then I don't *demean* it either. I guess I just *ignore* it, take it for granted. After all, didn't Jesus say we should give no thought to the body and what we wear?"

Well, yes and no. What Jesus said was that we should not be anxious or worried about feeding and clothing the body, for our heavenly Father will care for us (Matt. 6:25–33). But Jesus never said, and the Scriptures nowhere intimate, that the body is *unimportant.* "Isn't the body more important than clothes?" Jesus asked in the same passage (v. 25). The point is that the body is *more* important than material things and *less* important than spiritual matters of the kingdom of God, to be sought *first,* according to Matthew 6:33. The first step toward physical self-discipline is to view the body in the right perspective.

The three attitudes toward the body mentioned above—to *adore* it, to *abhor* and *deplore* it, and to *ignore* it—roughly parallel the three views of the body discussed by C. S. Lewis in *The Four Loves.* First there is the view, held by neo-pagans, some mystics, and nudists, that the body is glorious. For example, an ancient Eastern cult called the gymnosophists venerated the body. Such a neo-pagan view of the body is reflected in these lines from Walt Whitman's *Song of Myself:*

> The scent of these armpits aroma finer than prayer,
> This head more than churches, bibles, and all the creeds.
> If I worship one thing more than another it shall be the spread of
>   my own body, or any part of it.

As believers, we marvel at and praise God's wondrous creation of the human body, but we do not venerate it.

A second view of the body is that of the ascetic pagans, many of the Puritans, and some contemporary Christians. According to this view, the body is the prison-house or tomb of the soul or, as one Puritan poet expressed it, a "wicker cage" that holds the "bird of paradise," the soul. To others it is a "sack of dung"—"food for worms, filthy, shameful, a source of nothing but temptation to bad men and humiliation to good ones" (Lewis). One extremity of this view was expressed by a farmer in the Midwest when I was growing up. He used to say, "When I kick off, just throw my body to the hogs!"

Why and how has such a demeaning view of the body arisen in Christendom? Of the several possibilities, one is historical. In a number of Pauline churches (notably Colosse and Corinth) during the second century, heretical Gnosticism arose. One of its false teachings was that physical matter, including the body, was evil, despicable, and vile. A direct result of this belief was an utter disregard for the body, as evidenced by denial of resurrection, a strict asceticism, and sexual license. Paul warned the church at Colosse about "their self-humiliation and their ascetic discipline" (Col. 2:23 GOODSPEED) or "their policy of self humbling, and their studied neglect of the body" (PHILLIPS).

Also a part of the historical influence was the development, from the third to the seventh centuries, of the philosophy called Manichaeism. A combination of Gnosticism, paganism, and Persian Zoroastrianism, this heretical movement taught that there are two equally powerful, contending forces in the universe: good (consisting of deity, light, soul) and evil (Satan, darkness, and the material or physical, including the body).[1]

A second possible cause of the unscriptural demeaning of the body is a widespread misunderstanding of Paul's words in Philippians 3:21. The apostle emphasizes that our citizenship is in heaven, from which we eagerly await Christ, who will "transform our lowly bodies so that they will be like his glorious body." Rather than "lowly" or "humble," the King James Version renders the body "vile," that is, base, worthless, repulsive,

---

[1]Augustine early subscribed to this philosophy, but later repudiated it.

degrading, disgusting. (Almost as misleading is Phillips' adjective "wretched," that is, contemptible or despicable.) The body is "lowly" and "humble" in its mortality, but it is not "vile"—as if Paul shared the Gnostic and stoic contempt for everything physical. Perhaps this one adjective, carried over from the Geneva Bible of 1564, has done much to perpetuate the notion that demeaning the body makes one more spiritual.

The third view of the body, according to C. S. Lewis, is expressed by St. Francis, who called his body "Brother Ass." It's hard to imagine anyone either adoring or abhoring that scruffy beast of burden, the donkey. "It's a useful, sturdy, lazy, obstinate, patient, lovable and infuriating beast; deserving now the stick and now a carrot; both pathetically and absurdly beautiful." So it is with the body, Lewis says.

Lewis says further that "there's no living with it [the body] till we recognize that one of its functions in our lives is to play the part of buffoon." American poet Delmore Schwartz described the body in a similar way as "a stupid clown of the spirit's motive." But whereas Lewis applauds St. Francis' view of the body as donkey, Schwartz presents the body as "The Heavy Bear":

> The heavy bear who goes with me,
> A manifold honey to smear his face,
> Clumsy and lumbering here and there,
> The central ton of every place,
> The hungry beating brutish one
> In love with candy, anger, and sleep. . . .

Each of us has certainly felt beset by what seems "a heavy bear," an "inescapable animal [that] walks with us." Because of that lumbering bear, with its carnal appetites, "I do not do the good things that I want to do; I do the wrong things that I do not want to do." The apostle Paul cries out in utter frustration, "Who can save me from this doomed body?" (Rom. 7:19, 24 GOODSPEED). There is, of course, only one answer: "I thank God through Jesus Christ, our Lord" (v. 25).

The fact that we *have* bodies is "the oldest joke there is," C. S.

Lewis concludes. It may be true that the body is sometimes comical, even ludicrous—with its creaking joints and growling stomach, its thickening paunch and thinning hair. But neither our bodies nor the fact that we have them is a joke in a demeaning sense. Perhaps the initial step in disciplining the body is to realize why it is important.

The Body Is Important Because God Fashioned It and Values It

The best reason for considering the body important and deserving of care and self-discipline is that God fashioned it and values it. It is His creation—"fearfully and wonderfully made . . . intricately fashioned" (Ps. 139:14–15 MLB). God's regard for the body is evidenced, for example, by the archangel Michael's contention with Satan over the body of Moses (Jude 9) and by the fact that God Himself apparently buried Moses' body (Deut. 34:6). Our bodies are important to God, so much so that He has promised to resurrect them (1 Cor. 15).

The Body Is Important Because Jesus Assumed One

Most awesome of scriptural truths is that Jesus assumed a body of flesh and blood. He did not disdain our human form but, superbly self-disciplined, He took on mortal flesh with all of its weaknesses and frailties (but not its sin). Apparently the only man-made thing in heaven is the wounds in Jesus' hands and side—in the body He will occupy forever.

The very fact that the Second Person of the Godhead took on the human guise (Phil. 2:7–8), gives dignity to the human form. And the result of His doing so saves us from the penalty of sin; we are now being saved from the dominion of sin as we yield to the Spirit's control; and when Jesus returns we will be saved from the physical infirmities which are the results of sin's curse. Some day we will experience the redemption of our bodies (Rom. 8:23), but we are to be "redeeming" the body now, that is, buying up, through self-discipline, its opportunities for service.

The Body Is Important Because the Holy Spirit Indwells and Sustains It

Perhaps most astounding of all and the greatest claim for the dignity of the believer's body is the fact that the Holy Spirit has made the body His home. "You, however, are not controlled by the flesh, but by the Spirit if indeed the Spirit of God is at home in you," Paul told the Roman believers (Rom. 8:9 MLB). The very same Spirit who raised Jesus from the dead dwells in our bodies! And He has promised to give life to these death-doomed bodies (Rom. 8:11). This is primarily a promise for the future, at the resurrection, but it is applicable to some extent in the present. The indwelling presence of God's Spirit refreshes and sustains us in our physical weakness. In his letter to the Romans, Paul refers to the weakness of the flesh (6:19). Later he says that the Spirit helps or takes share in this same weakness (Rom. 8:26).

Perhaps you've had the experience, as I often have, of feeling completely exhausted, totally drained physically. But then you received spiritual renewal through prayer and the study of God's Word—and you also felt physically refreshed. I come home from work wishing for a good dinner, time to talk to the family, maybe read the newspaper or a good book—and then bed! But Wednesday evening is the time for the midweek prayer service at church. More often than not I *force* myself to attend—but ordinarily I come away refreshed not only in spirit but also in body as well.

The Body Is Important Because It Is the Seat of the Soul and Spirit

Our various faculties are closely related and interrelated. Consequently, the lack of self-discipline in one area shows up negatively in the others. For example, failure to deal with anger, fear, or guilt is often manifested in such physical disorders as high blood pressure, headaches, backaches, ulcers, or digestive problems. Emotional problems can cause compulsive eating, which may result in obesity and general lack of physical health. Psychosomatic ills, those originating in or aggravated by mental or emotional difficulties, further indicate the interrelationship.

Not only does lack of self-discipline of the soul and spirit affect the body, but the physical condition also affects the soul and spirit either negatively or positively. Lack of a balanced diet and proper rest may cause depression, irritability, or a short temper. How can I expect to be my sharpest for the Lord spiritually, mentally, and emotionally, if I begin the day without a nutritious breakfast and then for lunch gorge myself with junk food?

Benjamin Franklin, in his attempt to achieve self-discipline, defined temperance as "Eating not to dullness." All of us know from experience that *what* we eat, as well as *how, how much,* and *how often,* affects how we think and feel. Overindulging makes us feel dull and listless. Jesus taught by word (Matt. 17:21) and example (Matt. 4:2) the discipline of fasting. Going without a meal or two (or more) can clear our thinking and help to discipline the soul. David said, "I humbled myself with fasting" (Ps. 35:13). Have we ever been so burdened with someone's spiritual need that we had no desire to eat and then, like Jesus at the well with the Samaritan woman, we had no *need* for physical food (John 4:31–34)? Can we say, as Jesus did, "My food is to do the will of him who sent me and to finish his work" (John 4:34)?

Because the body is the seat of the spirit and soul, it is the battleground, the arena, of spiritual activity. It is through the body that evil from the mind and heart is manifested in action; it is also through the body that the graces of the Christian life are revealed in action. These mortal bodies, if properly disciplined, provide the means of glorifying God. "Glorify God *in your body*, and in your spirit, which are God's," Paul admonished (1 Cor. 6:20 KJV). What does it mean to glorify God in your body? To "glorify" (the Greek is the source of our word *doxology)* is to honor, exalt, praise extravagantly, cause a manifestation of dignity, excellence, or majesty. Our bodies should be a Gloria Patri, a walking doxology. They should manifest the dignity, the excellence, the majesty of God.

You may say, "Oh come on now, aren't you making excessive demands?" No, they're not *my* demands, and besides they are not our own bodies. Paul said, "You are not your own; you were bought at a price" (1 Cor. 6:19–20). The believer's body is God's possession by right of redemption. Our bodies are loaned to us for a short time so that the Holy Spirit, through our disciplined presenting of those bodies, might manifest the life of Christ to the world.

How else can the world see the glory of God if not in *our* physical lives? Just as Jesus, in a human body, revealed God to man, so believers, as sons of God conformed to the image of Christ, reveal the glory of God. Paul said that we "bear about in the body the death-marks of Jesus, so that by our bodies the life of Jesus may also be shown. In the midst of life we are constantly handed over to death for Jesus' sake, so that the life of Jesus may yet be evidenced through our mortal flesh" (2 Cor. 4:10–11 MLB). Is the life of Jesus being manifested in our bodies? Can we honestly say we glorify God if we excessively overeat, if we are flabby and out of condition, if we are not in control of our physical appetites?

Also because the body is the seat of the soul and spirit, what we do *in* and *with* the body will be the basis for rewards of believers at the judgment seat of Christ. Paul said, "We have all to appear without disguise before the tribunal of Christ, each to be requited *for what he has done with his body*, well or ill" (2 Cor. 5:10 MOFFATT).[2] Physical self-discipline will therefore play a significant role in determining the effectiveness of our present service for Christ and our future rewards.

Once we recognize the importance God has placed on the body and once we begin to shed the negative attitudes toward our bodies, the battle for physical self-discipline is at least partially won. We realize that the body is not an idol to be worshiped, nor is it a dilapidated old house unworthy of careful maintenance and

---

[2]There is justification for translating the Greek word *dia* as a preposition of means or manner—"by," "with," or "through" the body, although most versions render it as a preposition of state or condition—"in" or "while in" the body. Essentially, of course, the meaning is ultimately the same: being *in* the body means working through it, and only if we are *in* it *can* we work through it.

order. It may at times remind us of an obstinate, ludicrous donkey or of a clumsy, ever-present bear, but the fact that we *have* bodies is no joke.

Perhaps the best way to understand what God wants us to know about physical self-discipline is to examine the figures used in Scripture for the body. There are at least seven such figures, each providing insight into the role of self-discipline.

THE BODY IS A "SECOND SKIN" TO BE WELL-PLEASING

Paul uses a dual figure of tent and clothing to characterize the body. These two items share a common source of material—skins of animals. He writes to the Corinthians, "Now we know that if the earthly tent we live in is destroyed, we have a building from God, an eternal house in heaven, not built by human hands. Meanwhile we groan, longing to be clothed with our heavenly dwelling, since when we are clothed we will not be found naked" (2 Cor. 5:1–3).

Our current state is that of a camper "roughing it" temporarily in a tent. The word that the King James Version translated as "tabernacle" is the same basic word used by John in his statement that "the Word was made flesh and dwelt among us" (John 1:14 KJV). Jesus "tabernacled" among us; He "pitched His tent" in our midst. Because He did so, John continues, "we beheld His glory." Just as "God was manifest in the flesh" (1 Tim. 3:16 KJV), or revealed and made visible in human form, so the glory of God should show forth in our bodies. "The light of the knowledge of the glory of God [shone] in the face of Jesus Christ" (2 Cor. 4:6 KJV), and so it should be with us.

I'll never forget how, as a young college student, I was challenged by a man of God who said: "If you read the Scriptures intently for fifteen minutes a day, it will change the look on your face." What may seem to be an incredible claim can become a reality (even if only by softening frown lines). I took that "Scripture challenge" seriously and it changed my whole outlook on life.

Not only our faces but our entire bodies communicate to those about us, sometimes in ways we least imagine. Psychologists say the first six minutes spent with a new acquaintance are crucial in forming impressions. "The apparel oft proclaims the man," Shakespeare's Polonius advises young Hamlet. What proclamation does this earthly raiment, the body, make to those about us? What does our body language say about our faith? Does a personable appearance and calm, well-ordered conduct show forth the Spirit in our lives?

Self-discipline permits the divine glory that is within to shine out. But the process is not passive. Paul says, "We labor [are ambitious to do something; strive earnestly; use one's utmost efforts; exert oneself to accomplish a goal], that, whether present or absent [from the body], we may be accepted of him [be well-pleasing unto him]" (2 Cor. 5:9 KJV). There's nothing passive about that! The verb translated "labor" is the same one used in 1 Thessalonians 4:11, where Paul urges believers to strive eagerly to be quiet, that is, to live quietly and calmly and attend to their own affairs and work with their own hands. That's self-discipline at its best! When this is so, we are "accepted of him," that is, "well-pleasing," the same word used in Romans 12:1, where Paul urges us to present our bodies as a living, holy, *well-pleasing* sacrifice to God.

THE BODY IS A TEMPLE TO BE SANCTIFIED

Another significant figure used in Scripture to characterize the body is that of the temple, sanctuary, or shrine, in which the Holy Spirit dwells. Paul asked the Corinthian believers, "Do you not know that your body is a temple of the Holy Spirit, who is in you, whom you have received from God? You are not your own; you were bought at a price. Therefore honor God with your body" (1 Cor. 6:19–20).[3] One of the most powerful arguments for physical self-discipline is this: the believer's body, dwelling-

---

[3]Earlier in the same epistle (3:16), Paul asks a similar question. In this earlier passage, Paul is referring to the entire church, the Body of Christ, whereas in the later passage he is referring to the physical body of every believer.

place of the Holy Spirit, is God's possession, not only by right of creation, but also by right of redemption.

As a temple, the body is a *place for* and *means of* worship, not an *object of* worship. Just as we do not worship the physical structure of the church, so we do not worship the body. But we do respect the church building. We keep it clean and well-conditioned, and so we must do with our body.

It's significant that a major event near the beginning of Jesus' ministry and then again near its conclusion was His purifying of the temple. John's gospel records the first (2:13–22), the synoptic Gospels the second (Matt. 21, Mark 11, Luke 19). In both cases, Jesus found the temple turned into a mart of trade, with trafficking in sacrificial animals and money-changing being carried on in the outer Court of the Gentiles. Jesus took dramatic action, driving the desecrators out and removing the corruption. On the first occasion, in John's account, Jesus then drew an analogy between the temple and His body.

When Jesus purified the temple of Jerusalem He was justifiably angered by the prostitution of the synagogue: its purpose was for prayer and worship, but it had become a place of merchandising. The same is true with the temple of the body: its purpose is to bring glory to God (Isaiah 43:7 says, "I created [them] for my glory"), but so often it is corrupted and used for ignoble ends. Just as Jesus cleansed the temple building, so must we cleanse the temple of our body whenever necessary, and keep it from defilement.

Just as the divine Presence dwelt above the ark of the covenant in the Holy of Holies, so God's Spirit dwells within our bodies. We should be able to say, as David did, "I love the house where you live . . . the place where your glory dwells" (Ps. 26:8), for our body, like the temple of old, is, or *should* be, "the mansion of [his] majesty" (MOFFATT). In His temple everything cries, "Glory!" (Ps. 29:9), and in the temple of our body every member, every last cell, should shout, "Glory to God!" The songwriter Frances Havergal expressed the importance of His indwelling as follows:

Take my hands, and let them move
At the impulse of thy love.

Take my feet, and let them be
Swift and beautiful for Thee;
Take my voice, and let me sing
Always, only, for my King.

Take my lips, and let them be
Filled with messages for Thee . . .

Take myself and I will be
Ever, only, all for Thee.

Are our various members—feet and legs, hands and arms, organs, eyes, ears, tongue—functioning in coordinated, harmonious control?

THE BODY IS A LIVING SACRIFICE TO BE PRESENTED

Not only is our body the temple in which we offer the sacrifices of praise and service, but it is also the sacrifice itself. Paul wrote, "I beg you, therefore, brothers, through these mercies God has shown you, to make a decisive dedication of your bodies as a living sacrifice, devoted and well-pleasing to God, which is your reasonable service" (Rom. 12:1 WILLIAMS). Just as Christ gave Himself on the cross once-for-all as a sacrifice in death, so we are to yield our bodies as a sacrifice in life. Just as the Levites were consecrated to God (Numbers 8) to live sacrificial lives of service before the Lord, so we are to deny self, recognize the claims of Christ upon us, and present our bodies to live sacrificially for Him.

Although the actual presentation of our bodies as living sacrifices is a once-for-all act, we must continually put to death the *deeds* of the body. Paul wrote to the Romans, "We are under obligations, but not to the physical nature, to live under its control, for if you live under the control of the physical you will die, but if, by means of the Spirit, you put the body's doings to death, you will live" (Rom. 8:12–13 GOODSPEED). We need not be controlled by the body's base sensual appetites nor by its cravings, legitimate in themselves, but hindrances to spiritual effectiveness. Victorious control over both is possible *through the Spirit*. Ultimately physical self-discipline is *spiritual* self-discipline, for, as Jesus said, "The spirit is willing, but the body is weak" (Matt. 26:41).

A newspaper article recently reported on the increasing number of young people who gorge themselves with all kinds of food and then induce vomiting so as not to gain weight. The increasing number of such cases brings to mind the decadence of ancient Rome with its grotesque vomitoriums. I know of one such teenager who overcame the habit when he committed himself to Christ and became active in Bible study, prayer, fellowship, and campus witness.

THE BODY IS AN EARTHEN VESSEL TO BE SANCTIFIED AND FIT

Another figure used by Paul to characterize the body is that of a common earthenware jar or clay pot containing a priceless treasure. "This precious treasure—this light and power that now shine within us—is held in a perishable container, that is, in our weak bodies. Everyone can see that the glorious power within must be from God and is not our own" (2 Cor. 4:7 LB). The precious jewel of the gospel is held in a fragile clay utensil so that, by contrast, the surpassing power of the treasure may be seen to come from God. The idea is that of a foil, bright metal placed under a jewel to increase its brilliance—and by extension anything that through strong contrast underscores or enhances the distinctive characteristics of another.

Our bodies are clay pitchers in which the light of the world glows. They may be scratched or chipped or cracked, but they must never be dirty, for dirt will keep the light from shining forth. What is the condition of our vessels? Are they opaque (not letting light pass through) or translucent (letting some light pass through but diffusing it so that objects cannot be clearly distinguished), or transparent (transmitting light clearly and distinctly)?

Paul further uses the vessel figure in his admonition to young Timothy. "In any large house there are articles not only of gold and silver, but also of wood and clay; some for noble purposes and some for ignoble. If a man cleanses himself from the latter [both the contamination and the contaminated vessels], he will be an instrument for noble purposes, made holy, useful to the Master and prepared to do any good work'' (2 Tim. 2:20–21). One view of this passage is that the noble vessels are gold and silver platters and goblets for use at royal weddings and state banquets, whereas the lowly vessels are commonplace clay water jars. Or to update the imagery, the honorable utensils are the costly sterling silverware and Lennox bone china brought out for special occasions, whereas the lowly utensils are the cheap stainless steel and the plastic dishes you got free at the supermarket. But both sets are functional, each serving a useful purpose on the right occasion. Ultimately, of course, the outward appearance is not all-important; it's what's inside the vessel that counts. Which would you prefer—a T-bone steak on a plastic plate or a hamburger on bone china?

Jesus told the Pharisees to ''cleanse first that which is within the cup and platter that the outside of them may be clean also'' (Matt. 23:26). The point is that we are to have a pure heart in a pure body. How? Paul tells Timothy in the remainder of the chapter to practice godly self-discipline. We are to flee from youthful impulses of the body and pursue righteousness, faith, love, peace, gentleness, patience, meekness (2 Tim. 2:22, 24–25).

Physical self-discipline is suggested even more obviously in Paul's third use of the vessel as a figure of the body. ''Every one of you should *learn to control his body,* keeping it pure and treating it with respect, and never regarding it as an instrument for self-gratification, as do pagans with no knowledge of God'' (1 Thess. 4:4–5 PHILLIPS). These same two philosophies or lifestyles are still present today. One says: ''Indulge yourself! If it *feels* good, *do* it! Do what comes naturally! You only go around once in life, so ya gotta' grab for all the gusto you can get!'' The other says: ''Deny yourself! Abstain from carnal indulgence! Practice restraint! Exercise spiritual control over the physical!'' Which lifestyle is yours?

The implication of Paul's words is that mastery over the body is something to be learned. Self-discipline requires us to do what comes supernaturally. How can we learn to master our bodies in holiness and honor rather than in the gratification of our passions? Paul gives the secret in the same passage (1 Thess. 4): because it is His will that we be holy (v. 3), God has *called* us unto holiness (v. 7), and has given us His Spirit, who is holy (v. 8). Mastery of the body must come from the *inside out,* through the Spirit's control, rather than from the *outside in,* through a program or regimen.

Genuine self-discipline of the body is essentially mind over matter—the mind of Christ over the matter of our bodies. Why not begin mastering *your* body if you haven't done so? Find a form of physical exercise that meets your own personal needs—handball, tennis, jumping rope, or jogging. Most people are convinced of the benefits of regular physical exercise—weight control, increased energy, decreased likelihood of heart attack, relaxation—but few actually begin, and fewer still continue.

I was no different. I had jogged before, but had quit when I got a "traumatized knee," from running with inadequate shoes. But I knew that I felt healthier during those jogging days. My metabolism speeded up (as evidenced by faster-growing hair and fingernails), and early every morning five days a week my mind was mastering my body. So two years ago I bought some well-padded jogging shoes and a jogging suit, challenged a friend to run with me, and became a serious jogger.

It's essential to have the proper shoes and to begin slowly. I began by jogging until tired (which was fairly soon), then walking, and alternating until I built up endurance. I now jog comfortably (relatively speaking) for about thirty minutes, five days a week. Setting goals and keeping track of distances provides incentive. And running with a friend sometimes helps my mind get my body out of bed. I don't lay claim to having experienced the highly touted "runner's high," but the run exhilarates me and also provides opportunity for my mind to meditate on verses of Scripture and the activities of the day.

There are numerous physical fitness programs popular today, involving various forms of exercising and dieting. Some individuals find walking a beneficial exercise. Recently the "rebounder" has become very popular (a form of small exercise trampoline). The important thing is to find a regular, consistent form of exercise that will increase the heartbeat to at least 120 to 150 beats per minute over a period of about half an hour.

Many of the physical fitness programs are effective and admirable, but physical fitness is really only a part of genuine physical self-discipline. Paul said in 1 Timothy 4:8: "Bodily fitness has a certain value, but spiritual fitness is essential both for this present life and for the life to come" (PHILLIPS). The way to achieve physical mastery is to be controlled by the Spirit, who indwells the vessel; He, the Spirit of holiness, works outward to sanctify and control the body.

THE BODY IS A FOUNTAIN OUT OF WHICH LIVING WATER FLOWS

The outward working of the indwelling Spirit is also depicted as a fountain. The basis for the figure is two passages in John's gospel. In the first, Jesus tells the Samaritan woman at the well that the water He gives shall be a well, spring, or fountain springing up in her into eternal life (John 4:14). Later, at the Feast of Tabernacles, Jesus again uses the figure: "He that believeth on me . . . out of his belly [stomach, innermost self] shall flow rivers of living water" (John 7:38 KJV).

On the final day of the week-long Feast of Tabernacles, the priest took a pitcher to the Pool of Siloam and poured the water as a libation on the west side of the altar. According to Jesus' analogy, the pitcher—and by extension, the well, the fountain, the river bed—represents the body, and the water flowing forth represents the indwelling Spirit (v. 39). The image is perhaps closest to that of an artesian well, which continuously spouts water to the surface due to pressure caused by underground water draining down from higher elevations. Our body, which is but dust (Ps. 103:14), is the channel for the Water of Life and the power of the Spirit. A self-disciplined body is a free, unobstructed channel.

THE BODY IS A BEAST TO BE BRIDLED

James says that any person who is able to control his speech is mature and "able also to bridle the whole body" (James 3:2 KJV). The infinitive translated "to bridle" denotes holding in check, restraining, or guiding with a bridle. The implication is that the body, like a beast of burden, has abundant energy that must be harnessed in order to produce beneficial work. Without the bridle the energy is wasted or, even worse, destructive. The body's appetites also need to be restrained and properly guided—illegitimate ones denied and legitimate ones channeled to God-honoring fulfillment.

But what is the bridle of the body? It's the same as the light shining through the tent or the Shekinah Glory from the temple, the treasure in the earthen vessel, the water flowing from the fountain—the indwelling Spirit of God, who works through our spirits by the Word of God and the conscience. Just as the Spirit is "the restraining power" that restricts the activities of the mystery of iniquity (2 Thess. 2:7 PHILLIPS) until the church is raptured, so for the individual believer He bridles the physical energies and holds in check the appetites.

THE BODY IS A SERVANT TO BE SUBJECTED

A final scriptural figure for the body is that of an unruly servant being brought severely into subjection. Paul said, "I beat my body and make it my slave so that after I have preached to others, I myself will not be disqualified" (1 Cor. 9:27). In the context of the passage, perhaps the best rendering of the verb is "to discipline by hardship" or "to coerce." My favorite translation of the verse is this one: "I discipline my body and make it serve me, so that, while heralding to others, I may not myself be disqualified" (MLB).

Paul told the Galatians that he bore on his body the brand-marks of Jesus' ownership that distinguished him as a slave of Jesus (6:17). The apostle bore in his body the scars of persecution for his faith in Christ. Most of us will probably never bear such physical marks, but our bodies àre slaves of His nonetheless, and they should manifest His life (2 Cor. 4:10–11). Are we consciously aware each day of our bodies as slaves of Christ—living to serve and please Him?

Either our body is disciplined to serve the spirit and Christ, or it is undisciplined—in which case we serve *it*. "Who can save me from this doomed body?" Paul cried (Rom. 7:24 GOODSPEED). Here, of course, "body" represents the entire sinful nature. It may be that Paul was referring to the grotesque practice of punishing a murderer by chaining to his back the corpse of his victim until it literally rotted away. Is it any wonder that the apostle cries out with such anguish?

Elsewhere Paul refers to those who have made their bodies, bellies, or their fleshly appetites their god or their supreme object of concern. In the church at Philippi there were some libertines who had distorted Christian liberty into immoral license (Phil. 3:18–19). Similarly, in the church at Rome there were some who, instead of being slaves to Christ, were slaves to their own stomachs (Rom. 16:18). Like them, many believers today *live to eat* rather than *eat to live*—for Christ. How pathetic to be a slave of one's own midsection!

Paul tells the Corinthians, "Everything is permissible for me, but I will not become a slave to anything. Foods are intended for the stomach and the stomach for foods, but God will finally put a stop to both of them" (1 Cor. 6:13 WILLIAMS). Paul here sets down the principle of Christian liberty, subjecting it to the twofold principle of expediency or benefit and self-control. In the Greek he uses a play on words: "Everything is in my *power* but I will not be brought under the *power* of anything."

Paul is talking here about a form of physical indulgence we don't hear much about in evangelical circles: gluttony. "God has given us an appetite for food and stomachs to digest it," Paul says. "But that doesn't mean we should eat more than we need. Don't think of eating as important, because some day God will do away with both stomachs and food" (LB).

Eating is not an end in itself, but rather a means to other ends: gratifying our God-given appetite for food, satisfying our hunger, and nourishing our bodies. God certainly expects us to enjoy, with moderation, this sensuous experience. After all, He gave us our taste buds! And have you ever thought of the *spiritual* dimension of eating? It is a perfect symbol of fellowship. (*Companion* comes from two Latin words meaning "breadfellow" or "messmate," someone with whom you eat bread.) Jesus often ate with His disciples and others, as when He multiplied the loaves and fishes and when He prepared breakfast on the shore after the Resurrection—and He offers to feast with anyone who will open the door to Him (Rev. 3:20).

But Jesus always put eating in its rightful place. When the disciples returned with food after His conversation with the Samaritan woman at the well, He told them, "I have food to eat that you know nothing about. . . . My food is to do the will of him who sent me and to finish his work" (John 4:32, 34). Although Jesus miraculously multiplied the bread and fishes to feed five thousand hungry people, after fasting forty days and nights He did not turn stones to bread to satisfy His own legitimate hunger. What was the difference? Self-discipline made the difference: the first was the Father's will, the second wasn't; the first was sustenance for others so they could hear spiritual truth, the second was for Himself at the solicitation of Satan. Jesus could say no to food. Can you? Going without a meal or two (or more) can clear our thinking and help to discipline the soul, as well as the body (Ps. 35:13). Someone has said that the best form of physical exercise is push-ups—pushing up from the table.

If it's true that inside every fat person there's a thin person trying to get out, perhaps it's also true that outside every thin person there's a fat person eager to climb in! Why is it that so many believers always seem to be adding on to the temple? Can you and I really be effective examples of the believer (1 Tim. 4:12) if we are physically out of condition? Maybe it's time to practice some girth-control!

Gluttony, placed next to sexual impurity in Scripture (1 Cor.

6:13), is perhaps the chief of the seven deadly sins in exacting the heaviest physical penalties this side of the grave.[4] Someone has said there are five ways of sinning by gluttony: eating *too much, too often, too greedily, too expensively,* and *with too much fuss.*

The apostle Paul goes on to say that "the body is not intended for sexual immorality but for the service of the Lord, and the Lord is for the body to serve" (WILLIAMS). Our bodies were not designed for self-indulgence, but for the Lord and His glory. If we do not use our bodies to bring glory to God, we are misusing, and ultimately abusing, them.

If, among the seven deadly sins, gluttony and lust are most obviously sins of and against the body, sloth, also a sin directly related to the physical, is on the opposite end of the spectrum. Whereas gluttony and lust are sins of commission, of doing or acting, sloth is a sin of omission, of passivity. Sloth is a disinclination to work or exert oneself, laziness, neglect of duty. It is the disciples snoozing while the Master agonized in the Garden of Gethsemane (Matt. 26:40–45).

But sloth is so much more than ordinary laziness: sleeping at the switch, lying too long in the bath, putting off the writing of letters. It is slackness in the face of spiritual good or uninvolvement in the spiritual best. Accordingly, some of the most slothful people are those who *seem* to be the *busiest.* Saul Bellow, Nobel Prize winning novelist, has a character express it this way in *Humboldt's Gift:* "Sloth is really a busy condition, hyperactive. This activity drives off the wonderful rest or balance without which there can be no poetry or art or thought—none of the highest human functions. These slothful sinners are not able to acquiesce in their own being. . . ." If the popular concept of the word is illustrated by the disciples sleeping while Jesus prayed, this deeper, more significant, meaning is illustrated by the disciples later resisting Jesus' arrest, and then scattering like

---

[4]Of course, each of the others—envy, pride, covetousness, anger, lust, and sloth—is rooted in or manifests itself through the physical. The "deadly" sins, originally called "capital sins," are no more ghastly than others, but indulgence in them leads to or involves the sinner in numerous other sins besides.

frightened sheep. Judged by the popular notion, Mary, sitting at the feet of Jesus, might seem slothful, but judged by the deeper concept, Martha, busy and distracted, is perhaps the slothful one in that she is uninvolved in the spiritual best.

Inactivity is not necessarily sloth, any more than activity is necessarily indicative of physical self-discipline. Some believers are constantly moving, always on the go, hyperactive even in *good* things but unengaged in the spiritual *best*. The difference lies in the discipline. In fact, sloth in its dual sense (really opposite sides of the same coin) seems to lie at the heart of any lack of self-discipline.

The "don't-care feeling," as someone has described sloth, or the "don't-care-enough-to-do-anything-about-it" attitude, is the great enemy of self-discipline. To be physically self-disciplined we *must* care. We must care enough to "acquiesce in our own being," that is, to recognize the God-given significance of the physical and come to terms with our bodies. ("My body isn't much but it's what God gave me, so I'm going to make it the best I can by caring for it, keeping it fit, trim, and well-conditioned.")

We must care enough to make this tent well-pleasing to Him, to keep the temple clean, to present acceptably this living sacrifice, to keep the vessel fit, to maintain the fountain unobstructed, to bridle the beast, to refuse to be a slave of our bodies and show our bodies who is master. "The Lord wants to fill our bodies with himself" (1 Cor. 6:13 LB). Do we care enough to let Him?

11 / Exerting the Will on Jawbone Hill: The Disciplined Tongue

Young and old alike have marvelled at Samson's feat in slaying a thousand Philistines with the jawbone of an ass. But some modern-day Christians equal or excel that record in the regular course of their lives, wielding their own jawbones uncontrollably. Samson slew his thousand, but we have slain our ten thousands! When he finished—998, 999, 1000—Samson cast away the jawbone and renamed the site: "The place has been called 'Jawbone Hill' ever since" (Judg. 15:17 LB). Today it's a thriving subdivision—inhabited by those who have never learned to control their talking.

"Sticks and stones may break my bones, but words [or jawbones] can never hurt me." Right? Wrong! This trite saying expresses only half a truth, and half-truths are often more seriously misleading than glaring untruths. It's true, of course, that words, being signs or symbols in the form of puffs of air passed through the larynx, cannot fracture my clavicle as a brick thrown through my window can. Yet words, mere sounds and signs, are able both to "bethump" us, as Shakespeare put it, and to provoke a flurry of sticks and stones—or bullets and bombs. Our very words can hinder, hurt, or help the cause of Christ. They may not break bones, but they can break hearts and lives. A Japanese proverb says, "The tongue is but three inches long, yet it can kill a man six feet high." "The words of a talebearer are as wounds," Solomon wrote, "and they go down into the innermost parts" (Prov. 18:8 KJV).

Perhaps the surest test of self-discipline, the acid test, is whether or not you and I can control our jawbones—our tongues, our lips, our mouths. Ah yes, our tongues. Isn't that the first thing your doctor examines when you're sick? If it's coated, you probably have fever; if it's yellowish the digestion probably isn't right; if it's bright strawberry red it could be any number of ailments. Just as the condition of our tongues is an indicator of our physical health, so the tongue is an indicator of our spiritual health. James said that if a person "can control his tongue he can control every other part of his personality" (3:2 PHILLIPS).

TESTING FOR TONGUE CONTROL

Are you ready for the test? Get in front of a mirror. Now drop your jawbone and extend that three-inch, flat, muscular organ between your teeth. Now think back over the past week. Think of all the difficulties that flapping muscle caused: the cutting remarks you made to your spouse, the angry words of impatience directed at your children, the fawning words of insincere flattery directed to associates, the name-dropping and boasting, the gossip about a neighbor, the unkind words you directed at a fellow believer, the words of criticism your tongue let fly at a church meeting before your mind was in gear. Don't you wish you could recall those words as the automobile companies recall defective cars? But it can't be done. Once they're past the teeth, they're gone, never to be reclaimed. That's why control of the tongue is so crucial. Benjamin Franklin expressed it in *Poor Richard's Almanac* as follows:

> A slip of the foot you may soon recover,
> But a slip of the tongue you may never get over.

Even biting the thing won't bring back words that should never have been spoken.

What's that over there in the center of your tongue? An "X"? Do you have an x-rated tongue? How did *your* tongue react in that unguarded moment when you hit your thumb with the hammer? Or when that person you *thought* was your friend unleashed a scathing attack on you?

Maybe profane and vulgar four- and five-letter words are absent from your speaking vocabulary. But what about those common expressions which are compromised versions of the original forms—the so-called "minced oaths"? For example, do you use such "minced" forms of sacred names as *golly, gosh, goodness, jeez, gee, jiminy, jeepers creepers, gol darn, Judas Priest?* Do you realize that when in a moment of uncontrolled anger you tell someone to "go jump in the lake," you are consigning that person to the Lake of Fire? Nonbelievers are sometimes amused at the curious inconsistency of believers who are offended at profanity but who use toned-down forms of the originals. A linguist and graduate professor of mine at the University of Wisconsin has said of this inconsistency: "A curious exhibition indeed, of the human desire to sin combined with want of courage."

BIBLICAL HOPE FOR TONGUE CONTROL

Are we agreed, then, on the diagnosis? Our tongues need to be controlled. Their lack of control indicates a wider and deeper lack of self-discipline. What about the prognosis? What are the chances of recovery, and what prescriptions are required? Well, let's not just sit here with our tongues hanging out! Let's get started.

The Book of James has more instruction about tongue-control than any other book, except perhaps Proverbs. James presents the following argument:

Major premise: If you can control the tongue, you can control the entire personality (3:2).

Minor premise: But you cannot control the tongue because it is "an intractable evil" (3:8 NEB).

Conclusion: Therefore, you cannot control the entire personality.

Sounds like a grim prognosis, doesn't it? Let's try to understand the basic principles involved.

First, in what sense can it be said that control over what we *say* enables us to have control over what we think and feel and do and are? How can mastery of that little three-inch muscle have such far-reaching effects? Size, of course, is no valid indicator of importance. Further, James is saying that we are all guilty of stumbling—over our tongues. No one is so perfect, so mature, that he or she is guiltless of a slip of the tongue in anger or guile.

Even the most exemplary saints have at times lost control of their tongues. Even the apostle Paul, not realizing that Ananias was the high priest, berated him: "God shall strike you, you whitewashed wall" (Acts 23:3). How different is the example of our Lord, who alone is faultless in control of the tongue. He "committed no sin, and no deceit was found in his mouth. When they hurled their insults at him, he did not retaliate, when he suffered, he made no threats" (1 Peter 2:22–23).

The statement of James further implies that because the most difficult mistakes to avoid are those of the tongue, the individual who successfully controls that member has a Christian character that is well developed and disciplined.

But I think the verse in James has an even deeper, more significant implication. Tongue-control is a matter of life and death. As Solomon said, "Death and life are in the power of the tongue; those who indulge it must eat the fruit of it" (Prov. 18:21 GOODSPEED)—or, as Moffatt says, "the talkative must take the consequences." Solomon also anticipated James's words, "He that guards his lips guards his soul" (Prov. 13:3), and "He who guards his mouth and his tongue keeps himself from calamity" (Prov. 21:23).

James reiterated several other basic principles stated by Jesus. The tongue merely reflects the heart: "Out of the overflow of the heart the mouth speaks" (Matt. 12:34). What fills the heart spills from the lips. An evil source produces evil results and a good source good results. Shakespeare expressed the point well in *Much Ado About Nothing:* "He hath a heart as sound as a bell, and his tongue is the clapper; for what his heart thinks his tongue speaks.'' To use Jesus' metaphor, we don't get figs from thorns or grapes from a bramble bush (Luke 6:44). James 3:12 echoes the plant metaphor in adding to the necessity of a good source the need for consistency in our speech: ''Can the fig tree bear olive berries? Either a vine, figs?'' (3:12). James clinches the effectiveness of these rhetorical questions with the decisive statement: ''Neither can a salt spring produce fresh water.''

But doesn't this view that the tongue merely *expresses* what the heart *possesses* conflict with James' earlier statement that control of the tongue makes possible control of the entire personality? Wouldn't that be like saying we can change the tree by taking care of the fruit, or make the fountain produce sweet water by cleaning up the bitter water? Perhaps an answer to this basic question will also illuminate the minor premise in the syllogism above: You cannot control the tongue (because it is an unruly evil).

Both James and Jesus clearly indicate that what we say is determined by what we are. James implies that tongue-control is achieved only by achieving complete self-discipline. But James also says that no person can control the tongue. That's true and consistent with other Scripture: *man* can't but *God* can—and will if we permit Him to do so.

OUR WORDS CAN CONTROL OUR THOUGHTS

But there is another crucial point. Jesus said, ''What goes into a man's mouth does not make him unclean; but what comes out of his mouth, that is what makes him 'unclean' (Matt. 15:11). An undisciplined tongue corrupts the entire being! It's obvious that our words can blight or bless others and that we can be hurt or helped by the words of others. But what I have never heard emphasized in evangelical Christendom is that the words a person uses can also affect, for good or ill, the person who says them. George Orwell expressed this significant linguistic principle in his famous essay ''Politics and the English Language'': ''If thought corrupts language, language can also corrupt thought.''

Similarly, Benjamin Whorf, in *Language, Mind, and Reality,* wrote: "The forms of a person's thoughts are controlled by inexorable laws of pattern of which he is unconscious. These patterns are the unperceived intricate systemization of his own language. . . ." Stuart Chase, in an article entitled "How Language Shapes Our Thoughts" that appeared a few years ago in *Harper's,* observed that language "molds one's whole outlook on life," for "thinking follows the tracks laid down in one's language." Thus while it is true that our words reflect our state of mind and heart, it is also true that the words we use influence our thoughts and attitudes.

Does such language as "cool cat," "funky freak," "groovy guy upstairs," and "swinging superstar," when used to describe the Eternal Godhead, reflect a scriptural concept of Deity? Doesn't such language demean the user's concept of Christ and affect his attitude toward God? What a striking contrast between such undisciplined, sacrilegious language and the Old Testament Jewish reverence for the sacred name of Jehovah—even to the point of their refusing to pronounce the name. Today, no more than He was then, God is not "groovy" or "hip" or even "neat," and Christ is not a "cool cat."

Jesus stresses the fact that our destiny is a destiny of words. Christ taught not only that we are accountable for our words but also that words will be the very basis of judgment: "For by your words you will be acquitted, and by your words you will be condemned" (Matt. 12:37). "Words may be either servants or masters," wrote Bishop Horne. "If the former, they may safely guide us in the way of truth. If the latter, they intoxicate the brain and lead into swamps of thought where there is no solid footing."

The grim syllogism based on James' argument can be clarified by this one:

Major premise: Heart-discipline makes for tongue-discipline.

Minor premise: I can achieve heart-discipline through the power of the Holy Spirit.

Conclusion: Therefore, I can achieve tongue-discipline through the power of the Holy Spirit.

Major premise: Tongue-discipline makes for heart discipline.

Minor premise: I can achieve tongue-discipline through the power of the Holy Spirit.

Conclusion: Therefore, I can achieve heart-discipline through the power of the Holy Spirit.

We have discussed in earlier chapters how to achieve spiritual, mental, emotional, and physical self-discipline. We need now to consider what is involved in achieving disciplined speech.

HOW CAN WE CONTROL THE TONGUE?

In *The Canterbury Tales* (Manciple's Tale), Chaucer wrote:

> The first virtue, son, if thou wilt learn,
> Is to restrain and keep well thy tongue.

Similarly, the English poet Francis Quarles said, "If thou desire to be held wise, be so wise as to hold thy tongue." And the anonymous author of this quatrain gave similar advice:

> If wisdom's ways you widely seek,
> Five things observe with care:
> Of whom you speak
> And how and when and where.

Sound advice! Wisdom and virtue lie in controlling the tongue, but how can we control the tongue?

Throughout the Word of God, three major images or expressions are used to characterize our speech—not just the *tongue*, but also the *mouth* and *lips*. In some passages all three are used almost interchangeably: "The *mouth* of the righteous brings forth wisdom, but a perverse *tongue* will be cut out. The *lips* of the righteous know what is fitting, but the *mouth* of the wicked only what is perverse" (Prov. 10:31–32). Similarly, Paul, in stressing that the entire world is guilty before God, refers to all three as part of unredeemed human nature: "Their *throats* are open graves; their tongues practice deceit. The poison of vipers is on their *lips*. Their *mouths* are full of cursing and bitterness" (Rom. 3:13–14).

The three are sometimes depicted as working together as part of a unit, as in David's prayer of repentance: "Save me from bloodguilt, O God, the God who saved me, and my *tongue* will sing of your righteousness. O Lord, open my *lips,* and my *mouth* will declare your praise'' (Ps. 51:14–15).

Of the three terms *lips* is the least common and the most specific, whereas *mouth* is perhaps the most common, particularly in the Old Testament, and somewhat more general, sometimes referring to the throat, the palate, and the cheeks as well as to the oral cavity. *Tongue,* sometimes used to denote a language or dialect, often refers to the articulation of speech, whereas *lips* often conveys the idea of a door or gateway to the mouth—the first to move in preparation for speech and the last chance to cut off words before they issue forth never to be reclaimed. Shouldn't you and I pray daily as David did, ''Set a watch, O Lord, before my mouth; keep the door of my lips'' (Ps. 141:3 KJV)?

Each of the three words is described by vivid metaphors that convey power and the necessity and difficulty of its control. For example, all three are likened to an unruly horse or mule needing a bit and bridle: lips (2 Kings 19:28; Isa. 37:29), mouth (Ps. 32:9; 39:1), and tongue (James 1:26; 3:2–3); also wild, untameable creatures, (James 3:7–8). Two are associated with a raging fire: lips (Prov. 16:27) and tongue (James 3:5–6). The same two are compared to deadly poison: lips (Rom. 3:13) and tongue (James 3:8). The lips are a trap for catching birds and small animals (Prov. 12:13; 18:7), and so is the mouth (Prov. 6:2). The mouth is likened to a tree producing good fruit or bad (Prov. 12:14; 13:2), as is the tongue (Prov. 15:4). The tongue is compared to a sharp sword (Ps. 57:4; 64:3) and to a sharp razor (Ps. 52:2). As someone has said, the tongue is not steel, yet it cuts. If you have a sharp tongue, you may cut your own throat!

The tongue is also like a bow (Jer. 9:3) and an arrow (Jer. 9:8). And the tongue is like a ship's rudder (James 3:4), small and maybe not very impressive looking, but powerful enough to control the destiny of an individual. Surely James did not overstate the case: control the helm of a ship and you control the ship; control a horse's mouth and you control the horse; control your speech and you control the entire personality.

The Word of God provides some specific details on what disciplined speech is and how it can be attained.

A DISCIPLINED TONGUE/LIPS/MOUTH IS *SUBDUED*

Have you been looking for the secret of a meaningful, virtuous life? Peter offers the following prescription: "Whoever would love life and see good days must keep his tongue from evil and his lips from deceitful speech" (1 Peter 3:10). The single verb in the main clause of the original means "to restrain," "prohibit," or "cause to pause" or "refrain." Very simply, the idea is to restrain the natural tendency of the tongue.

Think of how much sorrow and trouble Peter would have spared himself if he had learned the secret earlier and followed his own advice. When Jesus foretold His death and resurrection, impulsive Peter rebuked Him, saying, "Never, Lord! This shall never happen to you." Jesus then said to Peter, "Out of my sight, *Satan*" (Matt. 16:22–23). When the tongue is not subdued, that is, put under the authority and power of God, it tends to flap for the Devil.

About a week later, on the Mount of Transfiguration, Peter impulsively proposed they build three booths on the mountain (Matt. 17:4). This time, God the Father rebuked Peter's impetuous suggestion, and the words are especially fitting: "This is my Son whom I love, with him I am well pleased. Listen to him." Peter was talking when he should have been listening.

Peter didn't learn the lesson easily. In the Upper Room, when Jesus began to wash His disciples' feet, Peter blurted out, "You shall never wash my feet" (John 13:8). Later Peter boasted, "I will lay down my life for you" (John 13:37), but later that evening Peter sinned grievously with his tongue when he denied Christ and cursed. Even after the Resurrection, Peter was the first to blurt out, "I'm going out to fish" (John 21:3), back to self-will and to fruitless efforts. And it was Peter who was quick to ask Christ about John's death, "What about him?" (John 21:21)—worrying about the other fellow.

Can't we see *ourselves* in Peter? But this impetuous man became a dynamic witness for Christ. What made the difference? Study his two epistles, noting especially what he has to say about *speaking*. He warns against false teachers who "speak empty, boastful words" (2 Peter 2:18). We are to get rid of all evil-speakings by craving the pure milk of God's Word (1 Peter 2:1–2). We are to follow the example of Christ (1 Peter 2:21–23).

We are to "always be prepared to give an answer to everyone who asks [us] to give a reason for the hope that [we] have" (1 Peter 3:15). To *silence* the tongue is not to *subdue* it. To be silent when we ought to speak out can be as grave a sin as speaking when we should remain silent! There is "a time to keep silent," for "in the multitude of words there lacketh not sin, but he that refraineth his lips is wise" (Prov. 10:19 KJV). But the author of those words also said that there is a time to speak (Eccl. 3:7). The subdued tongue, as illustrated by the example of Christ, will speak when it ought to speak and be silent when it ought to be silent.

Don't you think that if Peter's uncontrolled tongue could be subdued by the Spirit of God, yours and mine can too? They can—if we first recognize the danger of perverse lips. Then, yielded to the Spirit, we must, by an act of the will, purpose to restrain our speech. David said, "I have resolved that my mouth will not sin" (Ps. 17:3). "I will guard my ways, that I may not sin with my tongue; I will guard my mouth as with a muzzle" (Ps. 39:1 NASB). Then there must come the continuous prayer of commitment, such as the one David prayed: "May the words of my mouth and the meditation of my heart be pleasing in your sight, O Lord, my Rock and my Redeemer" (Ps. 19:14). This prayer ought to be daily on our lips.

A DISCIPLINED TONGUE/LIPS/MOUTH IS *SANCTIFIED*

Words acceptable to God assure that our tongues are sanctified.

The time is about 740 B.C. Uzziah, eleventh king of Judah, has died after a fifty-two year reign. The prophet Isaiah, in the temple perhaps to seek God's guidance during such a critical time, has an overpowering vision of God's majesty and holiness. His immediate reaction is to cry out, "Woe to me! I am ruined! For I am a man of unclean lips, and I live among a people of unclean lips" (Isa. 6:5 NASB). ("I am a foul-mouthed sinner, a member of a sinful, foul-mouthed race." LB) Isaiah's sense of guilt centers upon his lips that had spoken the language of a corrupt heart. Only when a live coal from the altar purged his lips was the prophet fit to go forth in service.

Whether this experience represents the initial call of Isaiah or a reconsecration for service, we do not know. One thing is clear: the condition of lip-impurity is universal and epidemic. The passage is reminiscent of Moses' experience when he was called to lead the Israelites out of Egypt. He replied, "I am of uncircumcised lips" (Exod. 6:30 KJV). It's not simply that Moses was a stammering, faltering speaker. Moses felt the need for sanctified lips—lips set apart and made holy. Just as physical circumcision was the sign of God's covenant with Israel, so symbolic circumcision means the special setting apart and the force of authority that accompanies it. Similarly, on the day of Pentecost, tongues of fire rested on the disciples as they were set apart to speak the good news. Jehovah promised Moses, "I will be with thy mouth" (Exod. 4:12, 15). I believe He offers that promise to us today. Let's claim it.

Have you ever found yourself about to give somebody a real tongue-lashing—but then you caught yourself and let God give you gracious words to say instead? One of my pet peeves is telephone solicitors—carpet cleaners, photographers, or realtors. One Saturday afternoon I was trimming a tree in the back yard. When the phone rang I remembered that the rest of the family was out shopping, so I hurried down the ladder to answer it. It was a friendly pest-control service. I *almost* gave him some choice words on "pests," but I caught myself. I believe the Holy Spirit helped me courteously reply, "No, we have no need for your services at this time, but thank you for calling." I am trying to learn to think first—maybe twice—before speaking and to give the Holy Spirit a chance to substitute gracious words for the impulsive ones.

When our tongues are yielded to Him, He sanctifies them; that is, He sets them apart for good things and makes them holy so they speak only the best things. Then you and I can say with Solomon, "Listen, for I have worthy things to say; I open my lips to speak what is right. My mouth speaks what is true. . . . All the words of my mouth are just; none of them is crooked or perverse" (Prov. 8:6–8). Can you make that claim? Does it sound like arrogant boasting? In our own strength it certainly would be, but when the tongue is subdued and sanctified, God controls it. Solomon gives further insight when he writes, "The heart of the righteous studieth how to answer: but the mouth of the wicked poureth out evil things" (Prov. 15:28 KJV). Two kinds of responses are described here. One is that of the unsanctified tongue, which spews forth a flood of evil words without thinking. The other is that of the sanctified tongue, which answers only after the heart has carefully weighed, pondered, and deliberated upon the best answer.

How should we give a reason to everyone for our hope? By sanctifying Christ as Lord in our hearts. When we revere and honor Him, He sanctifies our tongues so they will be ready to answer as they should.

A DISCIPLINED TONGUE/LIPS/MOUTH IS *SEASONED*

In order to answer everyone as we ought, Paul says, our speech should be constantly "seasoned with the salt of grace" (Col. 4:6 WEYMOUTH). The idea conveyed by the salt is that our speech should not be insipid—dull, lifeless, tasteless, flat, uninteresting. Our talk should be characterized by winsomeness, that is, charm, engaging attractiveness, and pleasantness. Someone has well said, "The way to win some is to be winsome." Knox translates the phrase "with an edge of liveliness."

"Seasoning" conveys several ideas. Discipline seasoned with kindness is correction tempered, softened, or made less harsh and severe. A speech seasoned with humor is one to which interest and zest are added. Seasoned lumber is made more suitable for use by aging and drying, and a seasoned actor is one whose experience has improved his performance. A person seasoned to a hard life has become accustomed to hardship through experience and maturity. Grace seasons our speech in all these ways.

Our comments, particularly those that are necessarily blunt, should be tempered with graciousness. I know some believers who maintain, "Well, I believe we ought to say exactly what we think and feel about anything. Let the chips fall where they may." Frankly, I once held this view myself—until I realized that God wants me to be candid, but with consideration and graciousness. For example, in writing letters of recommendation, in conducting personal interviews, in evaluating colleagues' proposals and writings, in participating on committees and boards, I believe God wants me to be straightforward—but in a gracious way.

Grace is that divine gift that takes an unpleasing circumstance and transforms it into a pleasing one. Grace in our lips makes our words *gracious*. Jesus perfectly illustrates the disciplined tongue as one seasoned with grace. One of the messianic psalms says of Him, "Grace is poured into thy lips" (45:2 KJV). And when Jesus began His public ministry by reading and expounding Isaiah 61 in the synagogue, everyone was amazed at His gracious words (Luke 4:22).

Do gracious words proceed out of our mouths? That's God's ideal for us. Solomon writes about the righteous man who has grace in his lips (Prov. 22:11), whose mouth is "a fountain of life," whereas "violence overwhelms the mouth of the wicked" (Prov. 10:11).

God intends us to experience grace every day of our lives (cf. Titus 2:11–13). We need to learn the secret of appropriating God's grace and applying it to our speech so it can change a potentially unpleasant or ugly circumstance into a pleasing one—even in those irritating, nitty-gritty situations of life. For example, a few weeks ago my family and I were waiting in line for Big Macs at McDonald's. Everyone in front of us seemed sullen and irritable, and when things didn't go smoothly, they gave the waitress a difficult time. When she finally got to us, she was so flustered she got the order all wrong. We were all tired and hungry—and the *natural* inclination would have been a verbal harangue. But God's Spirit provided gracious words: "Look, that's fine. I'd rather have a Quarter Pounder anyway—and the boys don't mind having onion rings instead of French fries. Say, I'll bet it gets tough working with hungry, impatient people all day, doesn't it? You're doing just fine."

She melted—right along with the cheese on the next Big Mac! She said, "You know, you're the first person who's really said anything nice to me all day. You're really a great family."

"No, it's not that. You see, we belong to God and He is helping us control our tongues."

I wish I could say I *always* respond with gracious words. I don't. But God is patiently teaching me. I could have told the young lady in McDonald's, "I'm glad you didn't hear me talking on the phone the other day to the drapery cleaning service!" ·

A DISCIPLINED TONGUE/LIPS/MOUTH IS *STERLING*

One of the most vivid images of the disciplined tongue in the Scriptures is that provided by Solomon: "The tongue of the righteous is choice silver but the heart of the wicked is of little value" (Prov. 10:20). Do you have a silver tongue? I don't mean silver-tongued eloquence and persuasive ability. I mean is your tongue genuine sterling silver? Is your speech in every way of sterling quality—pure, excellent, honest?

The psalmist provides a vivid description of the undisciplined mouth: the wicked man's "mouth is full of curses and lies and threats; trouble and evil are under his tongue" (10:7). Here are enumerated the five major tongue-sins: profanity (and vulgarity), lying (craftiness, deceptiveness), verbal oppression and threats, mischief (talebearing, rumormongering, gossiping, troublemaking), and boasting (including flattery). How does your tongue measure up in this catalog of offenses? Do you need to confess one or more and let the Holy Spirit deal with them?

God commands His people, "Keep thy tongue from evil, and thy lips from speaking guile"—an admonition repeated by Peter (Ps. 34:13; 1 Peter 3:10 KJV). Guile is slyness, craftiness, trickiness, deceitfulness in dealing with others. Elsewhere we are commanded not to deceive with our lips (Prov. 24:28).

One of the greatest abominations to our God is a lying tongue (Prov. 6:17), lying lips (Prov. 12:22), a lying mouth (Ps. 63:11). "Oh, but surely no Christian believer would deliberately lie or be deceptive." Would God that it were so. But the undisciplined tongue, even of a believer, is deceitful and false (Ps. 120:2–3).

Linguistic puffery has brought about the lie that is not quite a lie and the truth that is not quite the truth. The English economist William Bagehot said, "There are lies, flagrant lies, and church statistics." It's called "speaking evangelistically"—not quite telling an outright falsehood but embellishing the facts somewhat to give a more positive impression.

For example: "At the invitation, some thirty-five people came forward to receive Christ." How many is *"some* thirty-five"? (Careful checking later showed that thirty-three actually came forward—perhaps the other two were counselors. Of the thirty-three, five wished to "renew their fellowship with the Lord," eight came to join the local church, two came to "dedicate their lives to the Lord," one came to make "a public stand," and seventeen came to "make first-time decisions for Christ.")

Another example: "An overflow crowd of over 1,800 was in attendance." (Police estimate: 1,200.) A church ad states: "Your friendly neighborhood church is just a few short miles off the freeway, just a few short minutes from practically anywhere in the Valley." Ours, you see, is an age of relativity, although the pastor probably preaches absolutes in the pulpit. Think of it! The miles to this church are not restricted to 1,609.35 meters each, and Ptolemy's minute can be shortened as one drives there! A religious breakthrough has come! If Madison Avenue can advertise "a larger pint," "a big, big gallon," and "a full quart," why can't Christians advertise short miles, short minutes, a full gospel, and a full salvation—as well as "an eternity that's gonna last a long, long time"? "Truthful lips"—the sterling lip— "endure forever," Solomon said, "but a lying tongue lasts only a moment" (Prov. 12:19).

THE DISCIPLINED TONGUE/LIPS/MOUTH IS
A *SINGLE* ONE

The genuinely self-disciplined believer does not speak with a "forked tongue" or with a double tongue, that is, saying one thing and doing another or saying one thing at one time to one person and another at another time or to another person. One of the requisites the apostle Paul sets down for spiritual leaders is that they be straightforward in their talk, "not shifty and double talkers but sincere in what they say" (1 Tim. 3:8 AMPLIFIED).

The double tongue goes right along with the double heart and double mind. The psalmist wrote, "They speak vanity every one with his neighbor: with flattering lips and a double heart do they speak" (Ps. 12:2 KJV). They say one thing but think and feel another. How often we're like the man at church who greeted a couple effusively: "Oh my dear brother and sister, we've missed you. We think about you a lot, you know, and we pray for you every day!"—after which he turned to his wife and whispered, "What *is* their name anyway? I just can't seem to place them."

The Scripture speaks about false words that belie true feelings. David wrote, "His speech is smooth as butter, yet war is in his heart; his words are more soothing than oil, yet they are drawn swords" (Ps. 55:21). And Jesus quotes Isaiah's prophecy about hypocrites who honor Christ with their mouth, but whose heart is far from Him (Isa. 29:13; Matt. 15:8). Is there a doubleness in what I say? Do people know that when I say something it's genuine, true, honest? Am I a man of my word? Do I keep my verbal commitments? There's no place in a Christian's life for use of the double tongue.

A DISCIPLINED TONGUE/LIPS/MOUTH IS
SOFT AND *SWEET*

There's nothing quite so pleasant as a sweet tongue. Not a sweet tooth but a sweet tongue is a mark of self-discipline. It always has a considerate word of kindness—even in response to bitterness. Do people criticize you and say nasty things about you and to you? Speak softly and carry a big honeycomb. Do your neighbors spread false rumors and gossip about you? Remember: soft and sweet. Do acquaintances and associates belittle your testimony for Christ, trying to provoke your anger? Don't forget: softly and sweetly.

To respond to verbal viciousness with sweet words is to go against the grain of our old nature, which says, "Blast 'em! Let 'em have it in return! No one's gonna talk to *me* like that!" To do so is to go counter to the world's thinking and expectation and practice. But as the Scripture teaches, "A soft answer turns away wrath: but grievous words stir up anger" (Prov. 15:1 KJV) and make things worse. The next time someone lambastes you, be prepared to hold your tongue until the Holy Spirit gives you an appropriate response. And if nothing fitting comes to mind, say nothing. Maybe the old method of counting to ten before blowing your stack isn't so bad. But while you're counting, ask God to provide a soft, sweet response that will turn away anger rather than fan it. The other person will probably be so flabbergasted he or she will be silenced!

Honey attracts and traps more flies than does vinegar. "Sweetness of the lips increaseth learning," Solomon writes. "The heart of the wise teacheth his mouth, and addeth learning to his lips. Pleasant words are as an honeycomb, sweet to the soul, and health to the bones" (Prov. 16:21, 23–24 KJV).

Young people often feel that if someone "tells them off" and they don't respond in kind, they are cowardly. But soft and sweet are not weak. In fact, the opposite is true. It's much easier to respond in kind than to go counter to our old nature and the way of the world. Solomon said that "a soft tongue can break a bone" (Prov. 25:15).

The Scriptures provide several beautiful examples of the disciplined tongue as sweet and soft. The perfect model, of course, is Jesus: "When they hurled their insults at him, he did not retaliate" (1 Peter 2:23). In Song of Songs, the bridegroom says to his bride: "Your lips drop sweetness as the honeycomb, my bride; milk and honey are under your tongue" (4:11). How different it is to have milk and honey under the tongue than to have "poison of vipers on their lips" (Ps. 140:3), "their mouths full of cursing and bitterness" (Rom. 3:13), and the tongue "full of deadly poison" (James 3:8).

God's ideal for us is that we have sweet mouths filled with milk and honey. The apostle Paul spoke of it when he wrote: "When we are cursed, we bless" (1 Cor. 4:12). Meet abuse with blessing? Yes. "Damn braces; bless relaxes," the poet William Blake wrote. And it does. To respond with sweet, soft words of blessing relaxes not only the tension of the situation but the speaker as well.

Solomon's beautiful portrait of the virtuous woman (unfortunately relegated almost exclusively to Mother's Day) includes as part of her exemplary character a sweet, disciplined tongue: "She opens her mouth with wisdom, and in her tongue is the law of kindness" (Prov. 31:26 KJV). Perhaps you've known such a woman—maybe your own mother or grandmother. My mother was such a one. She was quiet, soft-spoken, even shy, but when she spoke it was with wisdom, and her tongue knew "the law of kindness." I don't recall ever hearing her utter one word of profanity or vulgarity or complaint or deceit or abuse. The law of her tongue seemed to be: If you can't say something positive and uplifting, better not say anything at all. Such a law is scriptural: "Let no corrupt communication proceed out of your mouth, but that which is good to the use of edifying, that it may minister grace unto the hearers" (Eph. 4:29 KJV).

Want to have a sweet mouth? What have you been eating? Garlic and onions of Egypt? Uh-oh. It's going to take more time than a few Velamints. Try David's diet: "How sweet are thy words unto my taste! Yea, sweeter than honey to my mouth" (Ps. 119:103 KJV). Nothing will taste sweeter and sweeten your mouth more than the Word of God. Start the day with a Scriptural lozenge, and before you go to sleep at night slip one under your tongue.

One of the best examples of a soft and sweet tongue responding to violent anger is recorded in the story of Gideon. After God had miraculously used Gideon's three-hundred disciplined men to put the thousands of Midianites to flight, Gideon summoned troops from the other tribes to pursue the escaping hordes. The Ephraimites succeeded in killing the two high-ranking Midianite generals. But the tribal leaders were "violently angry with Gideon" because he had not sent for them when he first went out to fight the Midianites (Judg. 8:1 LB). They "criticized him sharply" (NIV), "reproached him violently" (NEB), "accused him severely" (MLB). Now notice Gideon's response. He said: "God let you capture . . . the generals of Midian! What have I done in comparison with that? Your actions at the end of the battle were more important than ours at the beginning" (LB). What a diplomatic response! And note the effect on the Ephraimites: "As he said that, their anger at him *melted*" (v. 3 MOFFATT). God can do the same with our tongues. Let Him sweeten them.

A DISCIPLINED TONGUE/LIPS/MOUTH IS A *SINGING* ONE

"Bless relaxes," Blake said—and as we are relaxed, our tongues are loosed to sing. Genuine self-discipline always has such a liberating effect. It never binds, restricts, or cramps our style; rather, it brings the freedom to enable us to sing, to praise God, in adverse circumstances. That momentous night when Paul and Silas were in Philippi the circumstances were anything but conducive to singing praises to God. The time was not favorable—midnight; the place was not favorable—a dark, damp prison; the situation was not favorable—they had been severely beaten and were now confined most uncomfortably to the stocks. Most of us would have grumbled, complained, felt sorry for ourselves, and blamed God. But here were two disciplined tongues which prayed and then sang praises to God. Most of us glibly sing, "O for a thousand tongues to sing my great redeemer's praise"— but we hardly use the one we have! We don't need a thousand tongues, only *one* that is genuinely disciplined.

David said, "I will extol the Lord at all times; his praise will always be on my lips" (Ps. 34:1). "Let us continually offer to God a sacrifice of praise" the writer of Hebrews says; "the fruit of lips that confess his name" (13:15). It doesn't take much discipline to praise God when the sun is shining and everything goes well. But what about the other two-thirds or three-fourths of the time—when the sun is hidden and everything seems to go wrong? Is your tongue disciplined enough not only *not* to grumble, but actually to praise God then?

God's ideal for His people is "the praise of God . . . in their mouths and a double-edged sword in their hands" (Ps. 149:6). Sing loudly and carry a sharp sword! The two-edged sword, which is the Word of God, and the high praises of God are closely related. With the Word filling our minds and hearts, we'll have praises on our tongues. David said, "My lips shall utter praise, when thou hast taught me thy statutes. My tongue shall speak of thy word" (Ps. 119:171–72 KJV). According to this passage, the Word is both the means and the subject of praise.

We learn self-discipline from instruction in the principles of God's Word—and praise is the result. When we practice devotional discipline and meditate upon our Savior—praise is the result. "My mouth shall praise thee with joyful lips: When I remember thee upon my bed, and meditate upon thee in the night watches" (Ps. 63:5–6 KJV). Is this your regular experience? Do you sing God's praises continually? Let God's Spirit instruct you in His statutes about tongue-discipline. Your experience will be that of David: "He put a new song in my mouth, a hymn of praise to our God" (Ps. 40:3).

Notice the glorious results of such a disciplined, singing tongue: "Many will hear of the glorious things he did for me, and stand in awe before the Lord, and put their trust in him" (Ps. 40:3 LB). Do the words *you* speak cause individuals to reverence God and put their trust in Him? If not, then maybe you need to let God teach you to discipline your jawbone.

Did you hear about the physician who tried to x-ray his patient's jawbone—but all he could get was a moving picture? You and I need to be still before God and let His Word x-ray our jawbones to reveal the flaws that need correcting. Then we will together glorify God with one mind and *one mouth* (Rom. 15:6).

12 / The Time of Your Life: Disciplined Hours

Imagine the following ad in the classified section of your local newspaper: "Lost: yesterday, somewhere between dawn and dusk, an undetermined amount of gold bullion in units of sixty ingots each." In small print are these words: "No reward is offered, because the treasure is irretrievably lost." A strange ad? Indeed it is, but one that each of us could probably take out in our own names. For most of us waste, squander, and lose, every day, sizeable amounts of that precious commodity—time. Rather than investing the 86,400 golden seconds of each day, we all too often lose them or merely spend them. And once they are lost or spent, they are forever gone.

In a sense, time *is* money, as the old saying goes—and, come to think of it, that's what some people pay their debts with! For others, time is what we are able to find or make when we really want to, but what we plead a lack of when confronted with that which we don't want to do.

Perhaps the most common alibi is: "I'm just too busy" or "I just don't have the time." Probably somewhere, every day, someone is saying: "Sure, Pastor, I'd love to teach a class, but I just don't have the time. My job's very demanding, you know. And then there's my service club and the Jaycees and the PTA and the bowling club and the Zorch Club and the Veeblefetchers

Union and. . . . I just don't have enough days and nights in the week as it is!''

Or how about this one: ''I'd love to serve, but I'm involved in this discipleship growth group and I just don't have time for anything else.'' (Do you detect some irony here? ''Sorry Lord, I'm too busy growing and being discipled to serve you.'')

Of course, there *are* some occasions when it's legitimate to decline if a task demands of us what we can't providentially give. After all, it's part of self-discipline, too, to say ''No'' when a negative response is warranted. But let's stop fooling ourselves and face up to the truth: Our real problem may not be ''overcommitment'' at all, but lack of self-discipline in the use of time. One of the most serious misconceptions today is that *busy-ness* means *service* and that *super-busy-ness* means *overcommitment*. Frankly, I'm not so sure I *know* any ''overcommitted'' Christians. Oh, I know quite a few who are busy-busy-busy with a flurry of frenzied activities—so much so that they don't even have time for their families. But I think that's a *lack* of real commitment rather than ''overcommitment.''

Most times when we say, ''I'm just too busy,'' what we really *should* say is something like this: ''I have just as many hours in my days as anyone else, but I'm so undisciplined in my use of time that I don't seem to get much of anything accomplished. Seems like the busier I am and the faster I go, the less I get done! I wish I *could* get it all together, make better use of my time!'' There's not a one of us who couldn't use some help in this area, not one of us who couldn't use time more effectively.

I suspect that most of us feel like the frustrated writer who said, ''I spent the morning putting a comma in and the afternoon taking it out.'' Sometimes I feel as if I spend my mornings clearing my desk and my afternoons cluttering it.

At the end of a day I try to think of what I've accomplished. Often it goes something like this: ''Took the car in to be fixed, then ran Kenyon to football practice, getting back in time to run Kevin to soccer practice. Ran an errand for Wanda, then took the boys to their piano lessons. Went to a three-hour board meeting at church. . . ." Does that sound familiar? There's nothing wrong with being busy with such matters as long as our lives don't become so cluttered with running here and there that we don't accomplish anything for the Lord.

TO MANAGE TIME, LEARN TO MANAGE YOURSELF

In the last decade or so there has been no dearth of books and seminars—both Christian and secular—on time-management. It's not our purpose to reiterate here what the best of these have offered. Rather, I wish to do what, to my knowledge, none of the books and seminars has done. I will consider time-management within the context of self-discipline. How can we learn to manage our time effectively if we haven't begun to learn to manage ourselves spiritually, intellectually, emotionally, and physically? Actually, we don't manage or control time anyway; we manage or control *ourselves in time.*

Any effort to "manage time" outside the context of self-discipline of the total person is like trying to control the right front paw of a tiger while ignoring the rest of the beast. Before we know it, we are *under* the tiger's paw or in the tiger's jaw.

Some time-management programs make grandiose promises and sweeping generalizations. A common one is, "We all have the same number of hours in the day" or "Nobody has any more time than you do" or "Your clock and mine run at the same rate." This all sounds valid, but it usually has the effect of making us feel guilty because we aren't accomplishing all the things our neighbors are. Of course it's true that all of us have the same number of hours in our day. But it's also true that the time we have at our disposal every day is elastic. My neighbor down the street, who has ten children to support with an eight-to-five job, obviously does not have as much time at his disposal as does another neighbor, with one child, who lives on investments from an inheritance.

In addition to the variation in daily disposal hours, there is a wide variation in the number of days each of us has in a lifetime. Only the Almighty Himself knows the number (Ps. 139). Even if we reach the magic threescore and ten or if, "by reason of strength, they be fourscore years, yet is their strength labor and sorrow, for it is soon cut off, and we fly away. . . . We spend our years as a tale that is told" (Ps. 90:10, 9 KJV)—fleeting, frustrating, sometimes futile.

Someone has drawn an analogy between a lifetime and a day, using the hours from 7 A.M. to 11 P.M. At age 20, it's 11:30 A.M.; at 30, it's 2:00 P.M.; at 40, it's 4:00 P.M.; at 50, it's 6:30 P.M.; and at 60, it's 8:45 P.M. Our time is fleeting!

In view of this plain truth, Moses prayed what each of us would do well to pray regularly: "So teach us to number our days, that we may apply our hearts unto wisdom" (Ps. 90:12 KJV). "Lord, help me to take such careful inventory of my time that I'll be able to apply myself wisely to accomplish the tasks You have for me."

Has the truth of the shortness of life motivated you to make the most of every opportunity? Carl Sandburg said, "Time is the sandpile we run our fingers in." That may be so, but some people have their heads in the sand too! They are whiling away their lives: "I'll do that in a little while"; "In a while now, I'll get organized."

The seventeenth century English poets wrote of *carpe diem,* "Seize the day." Robert Herrick put it this way:

> Gather ye rosebuds while ye may,
> Old Time is still a-flying;
> And this same flower that smiles today,
> Tomorrow will be dying.

Herrick's contemporary, Andrew Marvell, used another image:

> At my back always I hear
> Time's wingéd chariot hurrying near.

HOW I WAS FIRST DRIVEN TO SELF-DISCIPLINE

I suppose I first heard Time's chariot hurrying at my back most vividly when I was a graduate student at the University of Wisconsin. After having some tests made at the university hospital, I was informed that I was a diabetic. "Now there's no reason why you can't live a full, normal life—*if* you take care of yourself: follow your dietary regimen, take your daily insulin injections, monitor your control with frequent clinitests, get regular exercise, etc."

I got the message: If you want to live, practice self-discipline! That's a difficult message for a previously healthy and unrestricted twenty-one-year old to accept. But the alternatives were considerably less desirable. The doctor told me that diabetics face the likelihood of early death through complications. And he gave no assurance that such eventualities wouldn't ultimately occur even with the utmost of self-discipline. This news left me wondering what part would go first—maybe my heart? Or a kidney? Or my eyes? Or maybe a toe or two? I'm becoming too morbid, you think? Well, maybe you can understand why I need to number my days. You see, I *have* to be self-disciplined, like it or not.

But is it really much different with you or anyone else? Aren't we *all* under sentence of death? In fact, the appointment with death is already made (Heb. 9:27). Unless Jesus returns and takes us home without dying, it's only a matter of time for all of us.

Frequently since that March day in Wisconsin, I have asked God for more time, but then it occurred to me that I have no right to request more time unless I'm using the present time in the most effective, efficient way possible. And I don't think you have that right either. That's like singing about and praying for a *thousand* tongues when I don't make effective use of the *one* tongue I have. Why would God let me have more time to waste if I'm wasting the time I now have? God heard Hezekiah's anguished prayer and extended his life by fifteen years, but only because of the king's righteous commitment (2 Kings 20:1–6). Of one thing we may be certain: God has tasks for each of us, and He will give us sufficient time to complete those tasks if we are faithful to Him and use our time wisely.

MAKE BETTER USE OF TIME BY KEEPING
ETERNITY IN VIEW

I'm convinced that you and I can come to terms with time only through a commitment to eternity. A strong commitment is essential in any form of self-discipline—a commitment to God and His Spirit for control and a commitment of ourselves to the rigors of genuine discipline. When the emotion and glamor wear off, only the commitment will carry us through consistently.

We are necessarily creatures of time, but our commitment to its proper use must go beyond mere mechanical time to eternity. Our commitment must be in time but *sub specie aeternitatis,* "under the aspect of eternity" or "with eternity's values in view" or "with reference to eternal implications." It's only the eternal values that give time meaning. And in a real sense we live in time to prepare for eternity. Contemporary poet Robert Penn Warren has expressed it this way in his poem "Bearded Oaks":

> We live in time so little time
> And we learn all so painfully,
> That we may spare this hour's term
> To practice for eternity.

Perhaps we could say that time is best used that most prepares us for eternity.

Unless we have that basic commitment to eternity, we may be ever so busy making time (a curious, impossible phrase), saving time, on time, even ahead of time, but the flurry of activity will be meaningless.

Suppose you're flying from Los Angeles to Minneapolis. Shortly after the plane is airborne, the pilot's voice comes over the loudspeaker: "Good afternoon, ladies and gentlemen. Welcome to Flamingo Airlines Flight 85. I have some good news and bad news for you. First, the bad. We're lost. According to my calculations we should be over the Rockies, but it looks as if we're over the Pacific Ocean. There's no cause for alarm. Our flight crew will have this inconvenience rectified momentarily. Now the good news. We're making excellent time!" Isn't that a picture of many individuals today? They're lost, with no sense of purpose, no direction, no understanding of where they're headed—but they're making excellent time!

We can even go a step further. Some people, even Christians, have a sense of purpose and a set of goals, but they're all the wrong ones; they're not *God's* will and purposes. In that case, it is senseless to study time-management in an effort to make haste in the wrong direction. If you're on the wrong train, every station is the wrong station—regardless of how fast the train gets there. If your destination is Philadelphia, it doesn't matter how much time you gain and save on the way to Atlanta.

Do you continually hear that voice behind you saying, "This is the way; walk in it" (Isa. 30:21)? "The king's business is urgent," as David said (1 Sam. 21:8), but we should be certain it is the King's business we are about before we hasten to do it. Isn't it interesting that the command is to walk, not run? One of the common metaphors of the Christian life is the walk, not a dash, a scamper, or a scurry. Nor is it a saunter, a ramble, a stroll, or a shuffle. Walk suggests a deliberate, steady, consistent, moderate pace involving definite progression.

JESUS WAS ALWAYS "ON TIME"

Jesus, our example, manifested perfect self-discipline in the use of time. Though He is the eternal Son of God, He was born in the fullness of time (Gal. 4:4). He clearly operated according to a definite timetable, often stating that His hour had not yet come. Yet He was never victimized by mechanical time. There is no reference in Scripture to His running, yet He sensed the urgency of passing time (John 4:35).

Summoned to Bethany when His friend Lazarus was sick, He waited two days before starting out and arrived four days after Lazarus had died. It appeared that He was late (the time-management experts would no doubt say He was "irresponsibly dilatory"), but He wasn't. He kept perfect time. His seemingly late arrival, like the sickness itself and subsequent death, were "for God's glory" (John 11:4). The principle here is that you and

I, controlled by the Spirit of God as Jesus was, should use our time in such a way as to bring the greatest glory to God—even if we go against the best human advice of the day.

On another occasion, an influential ruler of the synagogue urged Jesus to come immediately to heal his daughter who lay dying (Mark 5:23). Now the efficiency experts would have advised Jesus to go quickly and directly to Jairus's house—and *then* come back and tend to the woman in the crowd. "Finish one task at a time!" "Follow through!" "Don't let yourself be distracted!" "It's only *logical* that since the little girl is more critically ill and is dying, you should go there first. Hurry along the side streets and if anyone tries to detain you, let the disciples handle it. You must learn to delegate responsibility. You can't do it all, you know. You're getting overcommitted. If anyone persists in detaining you, you've got to be firm and tell them you're too busy with a more critical case."

A *delay* in the case of Lazarus and now a *distraction?* Unthinkable! Oh, if only the Son of God had been able to benefit from our modern efficiency expertise, there's no telling what He might have been able to accomplish! If only He could have attended that two-day time-management seminar at the Nazareth Hilton. . . .

The point—and a very important point it is too—is that Spirit-controlled use of time may at times run diametrically counter to the human logic of efficiency experts. Can you imagine what the "experts" would have said about Philip's God-directed decision to leave Jerusalem, where he was apparently reaching vast multitudes with the gospel, and go south into the desert of the Gaza Strip, not even knowing about the one geographically strategic individual whom he was destined to meet (Acts 8)? "Now that's just about the silliest notion I've ever heard of! You're pulling out of the Greater Jerusalem Evangelistic Campaign and going to the desert? What a waste of time and talent. Be reasonable, Phil. Jerusalem is where it's at. That's where the people are. Are you bent on ministering to lizards? Look, if it's so all-fired important, why don't you send an associate evangelist? A cancellation in Jerusalem at this point is going to hurt your image!''

You and I ought to learn all we can from the best minds of our day, but we should also be so spiritually disciplined that we will go counter to their advice if God so leads. A case in point is a doctor friend of mine with impressive credentials: graduation with honors from Columbia University, medical degree from Harvard, thriving practice, the respect of his colleagues, and an outstanding Christian testimony in his community. But God spoke to his heart—and he gave up the lucrative practice and took his wife and three young children to the Third World, where he labors today as a medical missionary in obscurity and hardship.

I ask you—is he using his time and talent wisely? Many of his friends and even some of his relatives don't think so. ''Why, he could have stayed here in the States and carried on his practice, been active in the Christian Medical Society and his local church. He's just dissipating his time and talents out there!'' *Delay* and *distraction*—and now *dissipation?*

INVEST TIME—DON'T SPEND IT

The *best* way to use our time is *God's* way. And what is God's way? It's not to *spend* time, but rather to *buy it up* and *invest* it. Perhaps the key Scripture on the subject of time is Paul's admonition to the Ephesians: ''Walk circumspectly, not as fools, but as wise, Redeeming the time, because the days are evil'' (5:15–16 KJV). Phillips renders it as follows: ''Live life, then, with a due sense of responsibility, not as men who do not know the meaning and purpose of life but as those who do. Make the best use of your time, despite all the difficulties of these days.'' Paul gives the same exhortation to the Colossian believers: ''Walk in wisdom toward them that are without, redeeming the time'' (4:5 KJV). ''Conduct yourself wisely toward outsiders,'' the Modern Language Bible puts it: ''using your time to the best possible advantage.''

In the verses above, the verb ''redeem'' means to rescue or recover our time from waste or loss, then to invest it in purposeful, God-ordained service. Just as Christ redeemed us—in fact, *because* He bought us from the slave-market of sin—we ought to, and *can* with His help, redeem our time.

We are to redeem our time from all that would waste it, as a farmer drains a swamp or marsh and transforms it into rich, fertile farmland. I recall how as a youngster growing up, I sometimes watched farmers redeem waste or long-fallow land. Those who owned river-bottom land sometimes drained sloughs and cultivated that rich, loamy soil for a bumper crop of corn. Other farmers sometimes redeemed land by clearing trees, grubbing out stumps, burning debris, and then plowing and fertilizing. I learned an important lesson from all of that. To redeem anything is no easy task; it demands a workable plan for reclamation—and a great deal of sacrifice.

Maybe you have a segment of time that is producing nothing fruitful, or maybe it's being totally wasted. Maybe it's 5:30–6:30 in the morning. Have you been sleeping during that time? Or maybe reading the morning paper? Could you redeem that segment of time, reclaiming it for spiritual benefit? Maybe you could devote that time to prayer, Bible study, and meditation. Or maybe the segment is 10:30–11:00 in the evening, or part of your lunch hour. Could you buy up that time and invest it for God?

Or maybe you can think of hours or minutes during the day that you could redeem. We redeem our time when we invest it in such activities as providing honest livelihood; talking, playing, and praying with our family; doing good for others and edifying our brothers and sisters in Christ; sharing our faith with unbelievers; reading, studying, and meditating on the Scripture and communing with God; and honing our spiritual, intellectual, emotional, and physical self-discipline. In order to redeem time effectively, we need to be aware of what we redeem it *from*. There are certain thieves of time or, if you prefer another metaphor, stumps that must be rooted out if we are to reclaim the land for fruitful use.

DISSIPATION IS A THIEF OF TIME

"Dissipate" has a dual meaning: to break up and scatter or drive away, therefore wasting or squandering, and to overindulge to the point of harming oneself, wasting a great deal of time and energy on frivolous pleasure. Dissipation is the opposite of self-discipline.

Notice how both aspects of dissipation are illustrated in the parable of the Prodigal Son. The younger son, who wasted his substance in undisciplined living, scattered and wasted his goods and money, carefully earned and saved over the years by his father. He overindulged himself in frivolous pleasure until he ended up in the pigpen. Now that's dissipation with a capital "D"! But what we often fail to see is that his indulgent lifestyle wasted his time as well as his substance.

We aren't told how long the son was gone from his father's house (any while is too long), but Luke 15 includes several hints about the significance of time. "When he had spent all" (v. 14) is the "when" of dissipation. "When he came to himself" (v. 17) is the "when" of contrition. "When he was yet a great way off" (v. 20) is the "when" of reconciliation. The latter two took place in an instant; the former went on perhaps for many months and even years.

Some of us might be inclined to smugness at this point. After all, maybe we haven't wasted time and substance in riotous living as the younger son did. Well, there's no room for self-righteousness, because all of us have surely squandered precious time in frivolous attempts to find pleasure. And for those who still insist they haven't, there's the elder brother syndrome. Just in from the field where he was working, he becomes angry and refuses to join the homecoming celebration because he has served many years and has not, at any time, been disobedient. Well, that's admirable—and his father doesn't deny it. True, he wasn't off wasting time and money; he was at home busily serving, but from all indications, it was time-serving (Luke 15:28–32).

A "time-server" puts in his or her time, promptly punching the clock, but with no principles of higher motivation, merely making behavior conform to minimum patterns of expectation. With that kind of attitude, what good was all the older brother's busy-ness and time spent in the field? You don't have to go to a far country and live in sin to waste or misuse time. The believer who is self-disciplined in the use of time serves the Lord, not time, and does so because "Christ's love compels" him or her (2 Cor. 5:14), not because he or she is depositing years of good deeds in a spiritual bank so as to obligate God to send blessings. "I've been faithful in church for thirty-five years, paid my tithe, served on the board, taught Sunday school, gone calling. . . . I just don't understand why God would let this happen to me. . . ." Perhaps those who dwell most on their long years of service have been merely time-serving.

I think the saddest thing about the story of the Prodigal Son is that there is no indication that the older brother ever went in to the feast. Time-servers, like most clock-watchers, are ordinarily miserable, resentful people. They seem to think that spending lots of time is synonymous with using time wisely and that reward for service is based on length of time spent.

PROCRASTINATION IS A THIEF OF TIME

The word *procrastination* (from the Latin *crastinus,* "of tomorrow") literally means "to put forward until tomorrow." Though we all may procrastinate occasionally, the person who lacks self-discipline *habitually* puts things off. "Sooner or later" is invariably *later,* or more likely *never.* It's seldom *now,* usually *then;* seldom *today,* usually *tomorrow;* seldom *immediately,* usually *next week;* seldom *this time,* usually *some time.* And anyone who claims that he or she does not occasionally put things off is putting us on! Surely one of Satan's cleverest wiles is "in a little while"!

Have you ever thought about *why* we put things off? Why do we put off until the last minute getting in that report, completing that assignment, filing income tax, cleaning out the closet, fixing the leak, renewing the subscription, making the call, writing the letter? Postponement until *later* of things we should do *now* is based on four basic conscious or unconscious illusions.

The first is the notion that the task is unpleasant, or more unpleasant than it really is, in terms of the effort, cost, or time required. Have you noticed that we seldom procrastinate if the task is pleasurable? Can you imagine a golf enthusiast saying to a friend, "I know I haven't been out on the course all year, but I *will* go one of these days. I really will. No, I can't make it Saturday. Too much to do around the house. Maybe the following Saturday. No, guess not. Just remembered that I have to clean out the garage. Look, we'll get together *sometime*. I'll call you."

A second illusion is that we cannot, or do not wish to, face up to the imagined unpleasantness of the task. Humankind cannot bear very much reality, T. S. Eliot wrote. Part of the unpleasantness may be a fear of failure. To be sure, the task may very well be difficult and unpleasant. But the imagined difficulty is almost always greater than the *real*. Furthermore, the difficulty and unpleasantness of many tasks are compounded and intensified with postponement. We need to consider the cost of putting things off. For example, if I hear a small noise in my car engine and just ignore it, I'm likely to end up with major damage and a *large* bill.

A third illusion is that by postponing indefinitely, the task will go away so we'll never have to perform it. Or we may delude ourselves with the notion that if we put something out of our minds and don't think about it, we're "off the hook." "What you don't know won't hurt you," because it isn't real. Such reasoning is nothing less than dangerous escapism. It carries the kind of pathos evoked by the boy who, squatting behind a narrow light pole, thinks he can't be seen because he can't see anyone.

A fourth illusion is that another time—*any* time but the *present*—would be better, that is, easier, more convenient. There are some believers who never "buy up" the time to serve the Lord because they're waiting for a "better" time. "I'll start sharing my faith when I finish this Bible study." "When I finish my degree I'll get active in church." "Just as soon as I get settled in my job, I'll be available." We're always going to get organized—next week. Who says next week is going to be any better? It may be even worse. Or who says there's going to *be* a next week? The ultimate illusion of procrastination is the presumption that there *will be* another time, another opportunity.

"Do not boast about tomorrow," Solomon warned, "for you do not know what a day may bring forth" (Prov. 27:1). The rich farmer in Jesus' parable (Luke 12:16–21) thought he had "many years," but God said, "This very night your life will be demanded." The warning of James is sobering: "Now listen, you who say, 'Today or tomorrow we will go to this or that city, spend a year there, carry on business and make money.' Why, you do not even know what will happen tomorrow" (James 4:13–14).

Remember Felix with whom the apostle Paul reasoned of uprightness, self-control, and judgment? His procrastinating reaction has a familiar sound: *"When I can spare the time,* I will send for you" (Acts 24:25 MLB). There's no evidence that a "more convenient time" ever came.

No more convenient time than the present will come for you either, for God works in the everlasting present. "Behold, now is the time of God's favor; now is the day of salvation" (2 Cor. 6:2). What a tragedy it is to waste the present by living in an uncertain future, to sacrifice *now* on the altar of *then.* This is not to say there is no place for *waiting* in our Christian experience, no place for a "holding pattern," no place for delayed decisions allowing time for prayer and meditation. That's part of self-discipline too, as we noted earlier. But if we *wait,* as in *procrastinate,* we sacrifice precious time.

As youngsters when we were in a hurry to go somewhere or do something and someone yelled "Wait!" we responded with a pun: "Weight broke the wagon!" The wrong kind of *wait* can break *your* wagon. Are you going to procrastinate improving your self-discipline? If not *now, when?* If not *here,* then *where?* If not *this,* then *what?* If not *this way,* then *which?* If not, *why not?*

MISAPPLICATION IS A THIEF OF TIME

A third thief of time is waste through merely spending it rather than investing it. We *spend* time when no lasting value comes from it; we *invest* time when we are engaged in God-ordained,

God-honoring activities—for anything which God ordains, He honors, no matter how small, and what He honors will have lasting value.

Time and energy misapplied are time and energy wasted. Moses, in a verse we noted earlier (Ps. 90:12), suggests that learning to "number our days" involves *"applying* our hearts unto wisdom." *Investing* time rather than *spending* it requires a concerted, conscious effort—and instruction from the Almighty Himself.

"Apply yourself!" We've probably all said it, and we've had it said to us. But what does it mean? It means to concentrate our faculties, our entire being, diligently and intensely on the matter at hand. This is surely what Solomon meant in his advice: "Whatever your hand finds to do, do it with all your might" (Eccl. 9:10). Or as Moffatt renders it, *"Throw yourself* into any pursuit." Throwing yourself into your work leaves no room for half-hearted, slovenly efforts. Paul gave similar advice to the believers at Colosse: "Whatsoever ye do, do it heartily, as to the Lord" (3:23 KJV). The word "heartily" means literally "from the soul" or "wholesouledly."

Have you ever honestly admitted to yourself, perhaps late at night after a difficult day, "My heart just isn't in this work"? If your heart's not in it, neither are your mind and will. Unapplied efforts mean misapplied, and therefore wasted, time.

We also misapply time when we spend it wantonly on activities that may be perfectly legitimate in themselves, but which pilfer time from more beneficial things. When "good" things steal time from the "best" things, they cease to be "good." Individuals who spend hours watching TV misapply time that could be used in reading a good book. But someone reading a good book could be misapplying time that should be invested in reading the best book.

DISTRACTION IS A THIEF OF TIME

Still another common thief of time, and frequently a cause of misapplication, is distraction. Success in time-management lies in setting realistic goals and then methodically setting about to achieve them. But when we allow other matters to divert our attention, we not only do not achieve the goals but we waste time as well. Jesus set His face "like flint" to go to Jerusalem and die for us (Isa. 50:7)—and nothing could divert Him from that goal.

The apostle Paul expressed his concern that believers should "attend upon the Lord without distraction" (1 Cor. 7:35 KJV). How it must have grieved Paul that Demas, mentioned twice as a faithful fellow-worker (Col. 4:14; Philemon 24), was later diverted by his love for the world and forsook Paul (2 Tim. 4:10). For that matter, John tells us that *many* of Jesus' disciples, unable to accept the "hard sayings" of Jesus, "turned back and no longer followed him" (6:66).

Not only individuals but entire churches can be distracted from the Spirit-filled self-disciplined path. "You were running a good race," Paul wrote to the Galatians. "Who cut in on you and kept you from obeying the truth?" (5:7). Their spiritual progress had been arrested by false teaching which diverted them from the truth. The verb translated "hinder" in the Authorized Version is a term which has either a military use—soldiers cutting in front of opposing forces and arresting their progress—or a sports use—an Olympic runner cutting in front of another runner and breaking his stride.

Phillips renders this verse: "Who put you off the course you had set for the truth?" This version suggests the "red herring" technique, which is often used in arguments and consists of the attempt to draw attention from a major issue by raising a minor, irrelevant, or false one. The name of the device comes from the practice of drawing a smoked herring across the trail to divert the chasing hounds.

Some believers progress well for a while, growing in the Lord by strides—but then somebody comes along with a "smoked herring" and off the course they go, after some new "exciting" cult or doctrinal emphasis. If you've been distracted from God's best, if you're off the trail of God's perfect will, then you're wasting precious time.

DISORGANIZATION IS A THIEF OF TIME

Does your desk, your office, your home, your life have a sense of arrangement, of design, with the whole structured in unified and coherent parts? The poet Walt Whitman observed that "everything in its place is good and everything out of its place is bad."

The spiritual ideal is also order. "Everything should be done in a *fitting* and *orderly* way," Paul said. "For God is not a God of disorder but of peace" (1 Cor. 14:40, 33). Disorder and confusion, whether in a worship service or in our personal lives, are not of God. Satan delights in turning every Babel ("Gate of God") into a babel, every Bethlehem into a Bedlam, every innocent funfest into a Donnybrook. If he can merely keep believers unorganized and disorganized so that we waste time and accomplish little for God, he's won the victory. That's why the psalmist prayed so earnestly: "Order my footsteps in thy word" (119:113 KJV); that is, "Take the rule and management of my ways."

Think of how much time we waste because we're *dissipated, dilatory, desultory, distracted,* and *disordered.* Beware of the deadly D's!

It's not enough, though, merely to ward off the thieves of time or, using the other metaphor, to grub out the stumps. It's necessary to have a positive plan for the investment of our time. There are at least five steps or stages in any such plan.

Analyze

Any effective plan for improved time-management must begin with careful assessment, a taking stock of where we've been, where we are, and where we want to be. Such an inventory ought to be made continuously: at the end of every year, every month, every week, every day. We need to evaluate how we've used our time and determine how it could be better used. We have only 168 hours a week with which to work. Most of us have to sleep at least fifty hours a week and work forty hours. In addition, every day we must eat, bathe, groom, commute, take care of household duties, have time with our families, have family and personal devotions, and so forth. Just to see where your time goes, try making a detailed chart, perhaps one resembling that found in Benjamin Franklin's *Autobiography*.

During the regular period of inventory, we should continuously ask ourselves if we have made the *best* use of our time and how we could better invest it. Such was the practice of the Puritans in the early days of our country. Note, for example, these resolutions about time which were made by Jonathan Edwards when he was a student at Yale University:

> *Resolved:* To live with all my might, while I do live.

> *Resolved:* Never to lose one moment of time, but to improve it in the most profitable way I possibly can.

> Never let me lose one minute of time, nor incur unnecessary expenses, that I may have the more to spend for God.

> Let me never delay anything, unless I can prove that another time will be more fit than the present.

The modern American has long since lost the art of such disciplined personal meditation. Perhaps it's time we got back to this practice.

The seventeenth century had a special name for this intensified living and use of time—*carpe diem,* "seize the day." We need to grasp every moment and use it for God's glory. We need to squeeze every drop from life's orange (or lemon). Years ago I cultivated the habit of ending each day, week, month, and year with a brief inventory of how I used my time, how I might have used it more profitably, what I really accomplished. The practice is often very frustrating and humbling, but I believe God has blessed this effort to maintain a sense of accountability of time.

Itemize and Prioritize

It's logical that since we have only a limited amount of time, we should be sure the most important things get first attention. But what *are* the most important things in *your* life? Have you ever sat down and worked out your set of priorities based upon your scale of values?

The morning question, What good shall I do this day?	5	Rise, wash, and address *Powerful Goodness;* contrive day's business and take the resolution of the day; prosecute the present study; and breakfast.
	6	
	7	
	8	
	9	Work.
	10	
	11	
	12	Read or overlook my accounts, and dine.
	1	
	2	Work.
	3	
	4	
	5	
	6	
	7	Put things in their places, supper, music or diversion, or conversation; examination of the day.
	8	
	9	
Evening question, What good have I done today?	10	
	11	
	12	
	1	Sleep.
	2	
	3	
	4	

Here's the way I see my own priorities:

1. My relationship to *God* (Spiritual)
2. My relationship to *family* (Domestic)
   (Spouse—children—other kin)
3. My relationship to *other people* (Social)
   (Brothers & sisters in the faith—unbelievers)
4. My relationship to *job and colleagues*
   (Vocational/Professional)
5. My relationship to *self-concerns* (Avocational/Recreational/
   Educational)

This has not always been the order of my priorities. For awhile, my profession was in first place; at another time, it was other people before God and family; and at still other times, perhaps more often than I would care to admit, self-concerns were uppermost.

Jesus, in His Sermon on the Mount, stressed the need for right priorities and clearly indicated the paramount one: "Seek for (aim at and strive for) first of all His kingdom, and His righteousness (His way of doing and being right), and then all these things taken together will be given you besides" (Matt. 6:33 AMPLIFIED). "As your first duty keep on looking for His standard of doing right, and for His will, and then all these things will be yours besides" (WILLIAMS). The implication is that if we put the first thing—spiritual relationships—first, the other things, including other relationships, will fall into place.

I have found this to be true in my own life. As a new professor just out of graduate school and concerned about university promotion and the "publish-or-perish" system, I was sometimes inclined to neglect church functions in order to work on another article or book. But I soon came to realize that when I put God and His work first, I was better able to utilize the time I spent on the other priorities. Isn't that exactly what Jesus promised in Matthew 6:33? If you haven't claimed that promise and tested it in relation to the use of your time, do it now.

Devise and Schematize

Once you've established a set of God-honoring priorities, you're ready to go a step further and plan some definite goals.

People who never set goals and develop a plan for achieving them are like Lewis Carroll's character Alice in *Alice in Wonderland*. When she meets the Cheshire Cat, Alice asks, "Would you tell me, please, which way I ought to go from here?"

The Cat replies, "That depends a good deal on where you want to get to."

"I don't much care where—" says Alice.

"Then it doesn't matter which way you go," says the Cat. "You're sure to get *somewhere*—if you only walk long enough."

People ask, "Would you tell me, please, the best way to do things to save time?"

An apt reply would be: "That depends a good deal on what you want to do."

"Well, I don't really know—"

"Then it really doesn't matter how you proceed."

There *are* no short-cuts to genuine self-discipline, and there is no way to improve the management of time without a clear sense of purpose.

It is instructive to note the difference between a *purpose* and a *goal*. A purpose is a general intention or determination. A goal is a more specific objective or aim by which a purpose is to be achieved. For example, it may be my purpose to be a better parent. One goal by which to achieve this purpose might be spending more time with my sons—taking them on camping and fishing trips, and playing ball with them.

As we have already noted, the apostle Paul had a clear purpose and goal in life. "One thing I do: Forgetting what is behind and straining toward what is ahead, I press on toward the goal to win the prize for which God has called me heavenward in Christ Jesus (Phil. 3:13–14).

It's helpful to make three kinds of goal lists: (1) long-range goals (career and lifetime), (2) medium-range (decade and yearly), and (3) short-range (monthly, daily, and sometimes even hourly). Get yourself a notebook and keep a detailed record of what you *must* accomplish, what you probably *should* accomplish, and what you'd *like* to accomplish. Spend ten or fifteen minutes a day planning. (Use a pencil rather than a pen to allow for flexibility and the inevitable need for change.) Set deadlines for yourself, and when you finish a task, cross it off. Doing so will give you a psychological boost.

It is very important that you set realistic goals. For example, don't plan more for a day than you can reasonably accomplish. To do so is to program yourself for failure. And if you don't accomplish all you've planned, don't berate yourself with guilt; rather, try to assess *why* you didn't. It may have been that the goal was unrealistic. Or maybe one or more of the time-thieves snatched the time away.

Organize and Mobilize

After setting realistic goals, we must have an organized plan for carrying them out. A good place to start is with the prayer of Moses: "Teach us to order our days rightly, that we may enter the gate of wisdom" (Ps. 90:12 NEB). Notice that Moses refers to ordering days, not years, or even months. Although it's important to plan ahead, we must learn to live one day at a time.

Most people have trouble at this point because they try to set their *entire life* in perfect order—over night. Begin realistically—maybe with your desk. Get that organized; then move on to your filing cabinet. At the end of T. S. Eliot's *The Waste Land,* all of Western civilization is collapsing: "London Bridge is falling down falling down falling down." The speaker, realizing that he can't restore the entire world to order, says: "Shall I at least set my lands in order?" You and I cannot organize the entire world or even all of Christendom, and God doesn't *expect* us to. But we can at least set our own house and lands in order. And as individual Christians around the world let God teach them order and self-discipline, Christendom can become the example of order it should be.

My *modus operandi* may not work for you, any more than yours would work for me. I use detailed planning sheets of things to be done, calendar appointment sheets, and a compact appointment book I carry in my pocket. My wife prefers using a box of three by five cards, on which she writes things to be done daily, weekly, monthly, and yearly (one item to a card). If an item doesn't get done, she merely recycles it; if it does get done she records a check mark and date. She spends ten to fifteen minutes every evening organizing her cards, recording her progress, and planning for the next day.

Improvise and Realize

It's important to plan and organize, but we don't need Robert Burns to remind us that "the best-laid schemes of mice and men go oft askew." Company arrives unexpectedly, someone gets sick, the phone rings and rings again and again. The self-disciplined person must be able to improvise graciously. That is, he must make necessary adjustments when unforeseen events disrupt the careful plans, and he must do so without frustration and despair.

The phone *will* ring, probably when you're the busiest. You might answer something like this: "Hello. It's really good to hear from you. Say, I've got ten minutes. How can I help you?" Then stick to the ten minutes. On the other hand, we should never be so rigidly structured that we cannot minister to people's needs because it might disrupt our plans for the day!

I can imagine that the priest and Levite in the story of the Good Samaritan had important ecclesiastical duties to perform in Jericho! I wonder how many believers hurrying to Sunday school and church or a board meeting would stop to help a person in need. The example of the heart attack victim who sat slumped over the wheel of his car on the shoulder of a busy Chicago expressway during the rush hour and all night, but was helped by no one until his family found him the next day, is an appalling commentary on our busy-ness.

Self-discipline also calls for spiritual improvisation, the ability to scrap all of our best-laid plans when unforeseen events occur and to allow the Spirit to make changes. To be organized as a genuinely self-disciplined person is not to be inflexible. The founder of a rescue mission work in Evansville, Indiana, had a favorite phrase, and it has stuck with me: *"Flexible* in the power of the Holy Spirit." *Organize,* but, when your plans are disrupted, be flexible enough in the Spirit to *improvise.*

Time, like faith and grace and life itself, is a precious gift from God entrusted to our stewardship. How *much* of it we have is not so important as what we *do* with what we *have.* In the Parable of the Talents, one servant had five coins, another two, and another just one. The first two servants wisely *invested* their talents and received the praise of their lord, but the servant who merely buried his one talent was condemned for his wickedness and slothfulness (Matt. 25:14–30). What are we doing with our gold bullion—losing some between each dawn and dusk, squandering some in undisciplined living, spending it on things that are temporal—or *investing* it with eternity's values in view?

CORPORATE SELF-DISCIPLINE

13 / Bent Twigs and Budding Rods: Self-Discipline in the Home

Most of us can remember the rhyme about the crooked man who went a crooked mile, found a crooked sixpence, bought a crooked cat, and lived in a crooked house. What we don't know, maybe because Mother Goose never told us, is that the crooked man married a crooked wife and in that crooked household raised a family of even more crooked children. If "crookedness" is a self-perpetuating trait in the physical realm, lack of self-discipline is even more self-perpetuating in the domestic realm.

Not only do parents who lack self-discipline unwittingly promote similar traits in their children, but such parents are unprepared to discipline their children in such a way as to instill self-discipline. How can we effectively discipline someone else if we haven't learned to discipline ourselves? I'm convinced that there *is* no genuine discipline unless it is rooted in the parents' self-discipline which, in turn, develops self-discipline in their children.

Perhaps the greatest flaw in the vast number of recent books on the rearing of children is the absence of discussion of the need to help children develop self-discipline. Externally imposed discipline is essential, and we need to know as much about it as we can learn, but it is, after all, only a temporary process. There comes a time, all too soon, when parents are no longer there to say, "Do this" and "Don't do that."

Genuine discipline gradually becomes internalized. For the Christian young person, discipline is assumed by the indwelling Spirit of God when He is in control, by the sensitive conscience, and by the well-developed Christian character. As stated earlier, a basic scriptural principle is that if we judge ourselves, we will not be judged (1 Cor. 11:31–32). So it's very important that children develop this built-in disciplinarian. But how *can* they if parents have never learned self-discipline, and if parents have never learned how to pass it along to their children?

Can you remember when, as a child, you first heard the voice of that internal disciplinarian saying something like this: "Now I shouldn't do that. Mother and father don't want me to do it. If I do, they'll get angry and maybe spank me. That hurts. And one time when I disobeyed, I burned myself." Weighing carefully the consequences of our actions through recollection of past discipline teaches a child self-discipline.

DON'T JUST BEAT THE BOTTOM— BUILD THE BACKBONE

The primary purpose of discipline, then, should be the development of an ordered, organized, self-controlled, self-disciplined young person. But it seems that a popular concept of discipline today is short-sighted. In the minds of all too many people, discipline takes the form of authoritative control to enforce current obedience and ensure submission to rules. When Johnnie or Mary disobeys by not taking out the trash, the parents seem concerned only about the immediate matter of compliance. When three yells from the family room have no effect, the father, in a fit of rage because his favorite TV program is interrupted, storms into the children's room to threaten and cajole until the job is done. Is this *discipline?* Or is it an undisciplined response to undisciplined living?

To label as "discipline" those acts of enforcement that neither exemplify nor develop *self*-discipline is like labelling as "education" the enforced rote memorization of isolated facts without training the mind where to *find* information, what to *do* with facts, and how they relate to *truth*. Genuine discipline is more than picking up a youngster, plopping the child down on the right path, and zapping him or her when wandering off the path. It's *teaching* the responsibility of *choosing* the right path. This is the principle of the scriptural promise, "Train up a child in the way he should go: and when he is old, he will not depart from it" (Prov. 22:6 KJV). Or as the Living Bible renders it, "Teach a child to choose the right path, and when he is older he will remain upon it." A child will remain upon the right road because the externally imposed discipline has developed a self-disciplined Christian character. Discipline is so much more than beating the bottom; it's building the backbone! The woodshed must lead to the toolshed and the workshop!

The woodshed speaks of negative action: "You've disobeyed and done wrong. This will help you remember not to do it again!" But the workshop speaks of positive action: "Here's how you can do it right!" As a boy of nine or ten, I was punished for "borrowing" my father's good saw and then leaving it out in the rain to rust. But I can also remember my father showing me, by example and instruction, *how* to use the saw, the drill, and the lathe.

THREE ESSENTIAL ELEMENTS OF GENUINE SELF-DISCIPLINE

The writer of Hebrews discusses two types of discipline—one that was concerned only with the immediate, and one that was concerned with permanent effects. Our fathers "disciplined us only a short time, as it seemed proper to them; but He does it for our good, in order that we may share His holy character" (12:10 WILLIAMS). A free paraphrase might be: "Our fathers disciplined us for their good—that they might have a peaceful life—but God disciplines us for our own good, that we might become self-disciplined as He is." Three essential elements of genuine discipline are taught here: Genuine discipline is for the good of the one being disciplined; genuine discipline has long-term effects; and genuine discipline results in the disciplinarian's very character being shared with the one being disciplined. If the disciplinarian is not self-disciplined and does not instill self-discipline in the one being disciplined, none of the three traits will be realized.

The Hebrews passage emphasizes the "afterwards," the "later on" of discipline. "Later on, however, to those who are trained by [discipline], it yields the fruit of peace which grows from upright character" (12:11 WILLIAMS). Or as the Living Bible paraphrases it, "Afterwards we can see the result, a quiet growth in grace and character." With much of what goes by the name of discipline today, there *is* no "afterwards"—except perhaps at best a Pavlovian conditioning. But discipline at its best, its highest, is not mere conditioning; it is training in self-discipline. This kind of discipline yields fruit to those who are *trained* by it.

The rod, symbol of power, authority, and discipline, is important in scriptural passages on the rearing of children. In fact, many people might be surprised to learn that the familiar saying, "Spare the rod and spoil the child" is not in the Bible. The closest equivalent is Solomon's statement, "He who spares the rod hates his son" (Prov. 13:24). But a question equally as important as "Do you bear the rod?" is "Does the *rod bear?*" That is, does the act of discipline bear the fruit of self-discipline?

David, writing from the perspective of a shepherd, could say, "Your rod and your staff, they comfort me" (Ps. 23:4). The rod of Moses and Aaron, symbol of authority over and discipline of as many as three and a half million people, later budded, blossomed, and bore almonds. The primary significance of the budding was the divine authentication of the Levitical priesthood and, by extension, its typology of the resurrected Christ, God's High Priest. But beyond its primary significance, the budding rod provides an apt picture of the rod of discipline that later bears the fruit of a strong Christian character. Can it be that the paddle or stick or hickory switch (when our sons were younger, we sometimes used a wooden spoon) can take root, bud, blossom, and produce fruit?

Sometimes the results of past discipline begin to bear fruit before our eyes. I recall how my younger son a few years ago did something wrong and then looked at me with those big brown eyes of his and said, "I suppose you're going to spank me."

I said, "Don't you think you deserve to be punished?"

And he said, "Yeh, I do. But *next* time I'll remember *before* I do it!"

Not only *can* this happen if we exemplify and instill self-discipline, but it *must* happen if discipline is to be effective and lasting. Daring to discipline is not enough; we must dare both to exemplify and promote *self*-discipline.

IT TAKES SELF-DISCIPLINE TO DISCIPLINE PROPERLY

What happens when discipline is attempted without self-discipline? Consider the example, mentioned above, of Johnnie and Mary, who have failed to take out the trash. The father's lack of self-discipline shows up in at least three ways. First, he's not in control of *himself.* When his three yells are ignored and he has to interrupt his favorite TV program, he becomes enraged and storms into the children's room. When we try to discipline while in a rage, we are likely to do more harm than good, for it is surely obvious to the child that we do not have *ourselves* in control. Think of the glaring inconsistency being dramatized to the child: "Dad is trying to control *me,* but he can't even control *himself!*"

I'm not saying we should never discipline in anger, as some child psychologists maintain. I have never been able to accept this notion. Anger, given certain provocations, such as open defiance, is a legitimate, even desirable, emotional reaction—as long as we can be angry and not sin (Eph. 4:26). As we noted earlier, Jesus displayed anger but it was always *under control.* On the other hand, rage is *excessive* anger *uncontrolled,* often leading to violence. Jesus never showed rage, and neither should we. I have known of even professing Christians who became so enraged they seriously abused their children. Most battered children, I believe, are the unfortunate victims of parental lack of self-discipline.

The attempt to discipline when we don't have ourselves under control can also have the psychological and spiritual effect of provoking our children to wrath. Paul warned fathers, "Do not irritate and provoke your children to anger—do not exasperate them to resentment—but rear them (tenderly) in the training and admonition of the Lord" (Eph. 6:4 AMPLIFIED). Like the author of Hebrews, Paul refers to two distinct types of discipline. One, marked by lack of self-discipline, "goads to resentment" (NEB); the other, grounded in self-discipline, lovingly, tenderly, controllably trains with the kind of discipline God uses with His children.

Note that lack of self-discipline in the parent produces (provokes) lack of self-discipline (wrath) in the child. There are various ways that parents provoke their children. The provocation might be caused by endless scolding and constant nagging, by over-correcting, by overly stringent demands, by refusal to listen to their point of view, by always being negative, by inflexibility, by refusing to forgive and forget, by never admitting mistakes and seeking *their* forgiveness, by demeaning them as persons or unnecessarily embarrassing them before their friends, by failing to manifest the clear distinction between our love for them and our hatred of their wrongdoing and disobedience.

The case of George and little Georgie Jr. stands out in my mind as an illustration of how parental lack of self-discipline produces angry resentment and, in this case, longstanding rebellion. George was a zealous Christian father who believed that discipline is best achieved by speaking loudly and carrying a big, big stick. He had a fiery, uncontrolled temper and would spank at the drop of a spat. When, at eighteen months, Georgie would not stop crying during a Sunday morning sermon, his father hoisted him down the center aisle of the church and in the back room administered such a thrashing that it could be heard throughout the entire auditorium. The huge welts on the boy's backside healed *almost* as fast as the strep throat which was detected the following day.

When Georgie grew older, his father habitually embarrassed

him before his friends, none of whom seemed to be acceptable to George Sr. George couldn't understand why his son dropped out of church activities at age twelve and attended only when threatened with "the beating of his life."

And today George just can't figure out why his son ran away from home at seventeen. "I didn't think I spared the rod. Maybe I didn't lick him often enough or hard enough. But you know the Good Book says train them up in the way they should go and when they're old they'll not depart from it. So I think he'll come back—and if not, I'll go after him with a billy club when I find out where he is!"

According to the latest report, George Jr. is into the drug scene. Although I've never heard his side of the story, I suspect that George Jr. was repeatedly provoked to resentment by his father's lack of self-discipline, until he was driven to unrestraint. His father's inability to control himself resulted in a son even more unable to control himself.

A second manifestation of the father's lack of self-discipline in the case of Johnnie and Mary is his failure to control the children. His utter lack of control is shown by the multiple yells from the family room, which are totally ignored, and by the subsequent threatenings and cajolings. A father in control of his children would have a prior understanding with them about obeying on the first command and about the consequences of disobedience.

Such an understanding is easy to verbalize, but difficult to carry out consistently. And that's where self-discipline of both parents plays a big part. Like all parents, my wife and I early encountered the problem of asking our boys to *do* something— clean up their room, take out the trash, feed the dog, practice the piano, come to dinner—only to get no response. So we discussed the problem in our Monday evening family council and agreed that on such occasions we would count to ten. If there still was no response, definite consequences would be immediately forthcoming. When the boys were younger, this usually involved a spanking. In other cases, it might involve loss of the weekly allowance, loss of TV privilege, or being "grounded" for a period of time. There was a clear understanding: if you disobey, you pay the consequences.

Finally, the father's lack of self-discipline is shown by the fact that he does not have control of the situation. A parent in control of himself, his children, and the situation will never need to threaten and certainly not cajole! The children will know whether of not the parent is in control and will, consciously or unconsciously, respect and emulate this trait in their own lives. On the other hand, if parental "discipline" is simply a repressive authoritarianism divorced from genuine self-discipline, the children will most likely be driven to resentment and away from a self-disciplined lifestyle.

THE FAMILY IS A TRAINING GROUND

I like to think of the family as essentially a training ground for the development of self-discipline. Parents are responsible for both exemplifying self-discipline before their children and instilling it in them. Ideally, each member, including parents, is developing his or her own self-discipline and at the same time, whether consciously or not, serving to enhance self-discipline in fellow members.

I have always felt rather sorry for an only child, because that one misses out on so many lessons in self-discipline. As I look back at my own childhood, I appreciate the training I had as the youngest of six children. I recall how during berry season my mom would often make two huge berry pies and cut each into four pieces. When my oldest brother joined the navy, there was one extra piece of pie eagerly craved by each of five children. Even the trivial matter of splitting a piece of pie five ways or taking turns or occasionally giving up one's rightful claim or curbing one's appetite taught us about restraint and self-control.

If the family is God's intended training ground for self-discipline, is it surprising that Satan is attacking the family perhaps with greater intensity today than at any other time? For if the home is disrupted and broken or if the family does not fulfill its function, many people may never develop self-discipline. With the accelerated breakup of the family structure, we are seeing an accelerated breakdown of self-discipline.

As we've noted, lack of self-discipline is not only a result of disruption and disfunction of the family unity but also a *cause* of that disruption. Thus another vicious circle is put in motion. Lack of self-discipline in family members causes disharmony and disruption which, in turn, may lead to complete breakdown that prevents the development of self-discipline.

Some readers may be thinking at this point, "My family is surely not perfect, but we're together and there seems to be some discipline. I can see the need for self-discipline, but what can I do about it? How can we as parents instill self-discipline in our children and enhance it in each other?" Good question. How *can* self-discipline be instilled in our children?

Self-Discipline Is Caught

In any corporate situation—home, church, school, business—self-discipline is perhaps best learned by personal example. The authority figure—whether parent, pastor, teacher, or executive—must consistently *practice* self-discipline, manifesting a pattern of self-control in action. In those common, ordinary, daily affairs of life when we're unaware that we're being observed, little eyes are scrutinizing us. If Dad or Mom acts and reacts without control week after week, month after month, year after year—how do you think the children are going to act and react? The best legacy we as parents can leave to our children is a legacy of godly self-discipline.

Perhaps the psalmist had something of this in mind when he wrote, "The lines [boundaries] are fallen unto me in pleasant places; yea, I have a goodly heritage" (Ps. 16:6 KJV). In a real sense, learning self-discipline is a matter of establishing boundary lines. It's a matter of learning where and how to "draw the line" beyond which we will not go. Stop for a moment and examine your own boundary lines. Note how many of them have been drawn after the manner of those in your parents' lives or drawn over lines actually established by your parents.

In my own case, I can think of numbers of examples. I have always admired my father's self-discipline in getting up early in the morning—5:00 o'clock or 5:30 at the latest. To sleep as late as 6:00 would be wasting the best part of the day! And surely I will never forget my mother's beautiful example of sweet reasonableness, and her remarkable tongue-control even in the most trying situations.

Just as positive attitudes have a way of begetting positive attitudes, so good habits of self-discipline tend to beget good habits of self-discipline in children. This truth is illustrated in the legacy Moses received from his parents. Even though Moses was raised in Pharaoh's court, the brief time his parents had with him was sufficient for him to "catch" by example their self-discipline. Two clauses in Hebrews 11 provide the basis for this conclusion. We are told that by faith Moses' parents hid their three-month-old baby "and they were not afraid of the king's edict" (v. 23). Four verses later we are told that by faith Moses, as a young man, "left Egypt, not fearing the king's anger." It seems valid to conclude that the spiritual and emotional self-discipline practiced by the parents begot the same in the son.

This principle of perpetuation works in the negative sense as well. Four times the Scripture reiterates the fact that divine discipline for sins of fathers continues down to the third and fourth generations of children (Exod. 20:5; 34:7; Num. 14:18; Deut. 5:9). Remember Abram's lapse of spiritual and emotional control in Egypt when he lied out of fear, saying Sarai was his sister (Gen. 12:10–20)? And do you recall Isaac's experience in Gerar (Gen. 26:7–11)? Like father, like son! Isaac also feared, lost control, and did *what?* Sure enough, he lied about Rebekah, saying she was his sister!

Have you ever found yourself asking such questions as, "What's getting into these kids today—they're so wild and unrestrained?" Could it be that they've learned their lessons well at home?

When Johnny was six, he saw his father lose his temper and smash the TV set. When he was eight, he watched his mother break a set of china by throwing it, piece by piece, at the dining room wall. When he was nine, he watched his father strike his mother during an argument. When he was ten, his grandfather drank himself to death. When he was twelve, his youth pastor was dismissed for immorality. When he was fifteen, he had a coach who often lost his cool, threw his clipboard, and cursed the players. When he was seventeen, his teacher, who frequently came to class tipsy or high, hit a student and was dismissed. When he was eighteen, his supervisor at work sat around chain-smoking and reading "girlie" magazines. When he was nineteen, Johnny was expelled from college for cheating, fired from his job for skipping work, arrested for assault and again for driving while intoxicated and again for possessing drugs and again for stealing a car and. . . .

"How can you *do* this to your mother and me?" his father demanded. "You never learned anything like that at home!"

"I don't know what today's youth are coming to," his mother complained.

"The youth of today lack self-restraint and self-control," the psychiatrist said.

"It's shameful the way young people carry on today," said the educator.

"Youth today are setting a pattern that is alarming," intoned the sociologist.

"Tsk, Tsk," said the moralist.

If there's one thing the adult world can't stand, it's a kid with no self-discipline!

Self-Discipline Is Wrought

The consistent practice of self-discipline, though it is essential, is not enough to instill it in children or other members of a corporate unit. After all, the development of self-discipline, like any other form of behavior modification, is not automatic, nor does it come about by a process of osmosis. Self-discipline must be carefully wrought, that is, formed, shaped, elaborated with a great deal of conscious effort.

It is highly unlikely that a child will learn *self-discipline* if he is never *disciplined*. One of the stories of the Old Testament most filled with pathos is that of Eli the priest and his two evil sons. Little is known about Eli, except that he was a good man, a pure man, but weak and indecisive as a father. He must have been at least spiritually, physically, and emotionally self-disciplined, for his priestly duties would have required that. But his two sons were undisciplined to the point of blasphemy. They gluttonously and forcibly demanded a portion of sacrificial animals for themselves, even before the fat was burned as the law required. And they committed fornication at the very door of the tabernacle.

Eli warned his sons of their shameful practices, but certainly not with the urgency their deeds warranted. The problem was obviously a longstanding one, for they were already grown men. The Scripture calls the two worthless, not knowing the Lord (1 Sam. 2:12). Apparently Eli had never disciplined his sons. His faithful years of service as priest are dimmed by the loss of his children. "His sons were bringing a curse upon themselves, and he failed to discipline them" (1 Sam. 3:13 MLB). He failed to restrain them. His sons were subsequently killed in battle, and when Eli, an old man of ninety, heard the news, he fell off his seat and died of a broken neck. Had he not died of a broken neck it might well have been a broken heart. What a tragedy it is to see men of God, living self-disciplined lives and faithfully serving God, whose own children never learn self-discipline largely because they have never been disciplined.

Alexander Pope, the eighteenth-century English poet, expressed the basic principle: "Just as the twig is bent, the tree's inclined." If the twig is not bent in the right way by a skilled, self-disciplined hand, it will grow crooked and gnarled. If it is not bent and tended at all, it will grow wild and bear no fruit.

According to Dr. Lonnie Carton, a child psychologist at Tufts University in Massachusetts, saying "no" to children at the right time in the right way can help them to grow, to acquire social responsibility, and to learn self-discipline. Dr. Carton specifies three "nos" that parents should use: (1) the "lifesaving no"— stressing the consequences of dangerous activities; (2) the "challenge no"—stimulating creativity and responsive effort to strive by saying, "It may be too hard for you, but you can try it"; and (3) the "convenience no"—reminding the child that parents and teachers cannot drop everything and put the child's interests ahead of adult priorities. Daring to say a calm but forceful "No" and enforcing it can help to develop self-discipline in a child. For example, "the convenience no" (I would prefer calling it the "priority no") can develop *patience* and the need to *wait*.

Several other "nos" need to be added for the believer. The counterpart of the "lifesaving no" would be the "spiritual welfare no"—a forceful negative response to any behavior that would be spiritually damaging to the child or anyone else. For example, Christian parents should have the fortitude to forbid their children smoking, because the habit is injurious, not only to their physical health, but also to their Christian testimony.

What might be called the "divine no" is a negative response to anything forbidden by God in the Scriptures. For example, I believe Christian parents should take a clear stand on the scriptural command against believers being unequally yoked together with unbelievers (2 Cor. 6:14–18) in marriage, business ownership, secret societies, etc.

Do you dare to say "no" to *your* children? If not, don't be surprised if they say "no" to you! Remember Eli. Things could have been different for him and his sons if he had said, "No!"

Self-Discipline Is Taught

It's important that children know *why* they're being punished, that they understand the nature and consequences of their wrongdoing, and that they grasp the basic principle involved so in the future they can discipline themselves. Further, it's important that we *take* and *make* opportunities to instruct our children in self-discipline. Remember Solomon's words: "Train a child in the

way he should go and, when he is old, he will not turn from it"
(Prov. 22:6). We are to train a child according to "his way," that
is, according to the child's *own unique characteristics.*

We must be sensitive in making provision for individual differences, in adapting the discipline to the child and situation. As
most parents realize, each child is unique, with a different temperament and different needs. These differences must be taken
into account both in disciplining children and in seeking to help
them develop self-discipline.

For example, although children with a choleric temperament
("hot, quick, active, practical, and strong-willed") usually have
a stronger tendency toward self-discipline, each of the major
temperaments presents its own unique challenge. The sanguine
("warm, buoyant, lively and 'enjoying'") will benefit from his
optimism and love for people, but will have special problems
with disorganization, restlessness, weak will, emotional instabil-
ity, and egotism. The choleric will benefit from his tenacity and
practicality, but he will have to control a quick temper and im-
petuosity. The melancholic ("analytical, self-sacrificing, gifted,
perfectionist . . . with a very sensitive, emotional nature") will
benefit from his sensitivity and precision, but will need to control
moodiness and pessimism. The phlegmatic ("calm, cool, slow,
easy-going, well-balanced) will be strong in efficiency, dependability, and practicality, but he will have to control his lack of
motivation, indecisiveness, and stubbornness.

It's important to realize, however, that there's a serious danger
in pinning neat labels on ourselves or on other people. Such a
practice is usually a popular means of avoiding thinking and the
effort of really getting to know a person. It gets us off the hook to
say, "Oh, I'm a sanguine (or my son's a sanguine) so there's no
hope of my becoming (or his becoming) self-disciplined." A
reverse fallacy is implicit in a remark made recently by a colleague who likes to classify people according to astrological
signs: "Oh, you're a Virgo, so you're just naturally organized
and self-controlled!" Naturally self-controlled? My colleague
was never so wrong! A Virgo I might be, with a melancholic

temperament, but I have to work just as hard (or, more accurately, I require the same kind of Spirit control) as all you sanguine Sagittariuses (or whatever). I may have an easier time with organization and analytical introspection (though I doubt it), but do I struggle with my fluctuating moods and emotional reactions! And I know the challenge of trying to raise phlegmatic and choleric sons!

The apostle Paul noted the spiritual self-discipline that first dwelt in Timothy's grandmother, Lois, then in his mother, Eunice, and then in young Timothy (2 Tim. 1:5). Surely this reflects the influence of teaching in the development of self-discipline in children of successive generations. Dr. Lonnie Carton has said that "self-discipline can be inculcated by reasoning on the child's level of comprehension."

Someone has well said that "the poorest education that teaches self-control is better than the best that neglects it." Daniel Webster said, "Educate your children to self-control, to the habit of holding passion and prejudice and even tendencies subject to an upright and reasoning will, and you have done much to abolish misery from their future and crimes from society." Even more important is the fact that you will have helped them to become equipped for the Master's use.

Self-Discipline Is Besought

To beseech is to ask for something earnestly. When was the last time you asked God to help your child develop self-discipline? Do you make a habit of praying with your children, entreating God to help them correct a problem in the lack of self-control?

Then we should put feet and action to our prayers by seeking self-discipline in our children. This can be done by admonition, by constant encouragement, and by positive reinforcement. We are commanded to bring our children up "in the nurture and *admonition* of the Lord" (Eph. 6:4 KJV). To *admonish* is both to caution, reprimand, or reprove mildly and to remind, urge on, or exhort. Don't we all need occasional warnings and reminders about self-discipline, as well as exhortation and encouragement? So do our children.

When you see your child react in a self-disciplined way, why not express your pleasure—and God's? Just last week, my older son displayed surprising restraint and emotional self-control when his expectations were not realized, whereas his brother's were. I stopped and told him I was proud that he had reacted as he did rather than fussing, pouting, throwing a tantrum, or in some other way losing emotional control. On an earlier occasion, when his reaction was not so well restrained, I pointed out how he might have responded—and how God and everybody else concerned would have been pleased. The idea is to stress the rightness of self-discipline through positive reinforcement (encouragement and praise) and to stress the wrongness of unrestraint through negative reinforcement (warning, reprimand, and discipline).

Self-Discipline Is Inwrought

It's essential that we help our children make self-discipline habitual, the norm of their behavior. This kind of lifestyle can be inwrought, that is, worked or woven into the entire fabric or pattern of everyday life by offering practical guidance. Paul told Timothy that the spirit God has given us is "one to inspire strength, love, and self-discipline" (2 Tim. 1:7 NEB). As parents we must help our children develop this spirit which inspires to self-discipline.

The key concept here is *practical application* of principles already taught. When we consistently *practice* self-discipline ourselves, we are doing this. When we effectively *discipline* them, we are doing this. We can do it also when we observe individuals out of control.

For example, one day as my two boys and I were waiting in a long line of traffic, an impatient motorist illegally passed on the right, cut in, and aroused the impatient furor of other motorists. The incident provided an opportunity to talk about patience, the silliness and danger of such uncontrolled actions and reactions, and the need for God's grace to make us forbearing in trying situations.

When children describe actions and reactions that happened at school, there's an opportunity to ask, "How do you think Wally *should* have reacted? What would *you* have said and done? How do you think the Lord would have wanted you to respond?" The same thing can be done when the family watches a TV show together or when you read a book to your children.

Each of these means of instilling self-discipline—by practice, by discipline, by teaching, by admonition, and by application— ought to be a consistent part of domestic routine. Anything less, I'm afraid, will amount to offering a stone for bread, a snake for fish, a scorpion for an egg—as Jesus' parable of parenthood has it (Luke 11:11–13).

If we finite parents can give good gifts to our children, how much more our infinite heavenly Father offers the best gift—the Holy Spirit and His power. It's not enough to give our children merely *good* gifts, such as food and clothing. We must give them the *best* gifts. Primary among these best gifts is a legacy of spiritual self-discipline. Such a legacy can be realized only through God's great gift of the Holy Spirit, who controls and disciplines believers and enables them to control and discipline themselves.

14 / Bones and Stones: Self-Discipline in the Family of God

Imagine the climactic scene of a beautiful ballet such as *Swan Lake*. The stage is filled with whirling, swirling, twirling movement. Kaleidoscopic patterns form, rotate, and then re-form. Individuals, couples, and small groups gracefully interweave, perfectly synchronized.

But suddenly we realize that there's something very peculiar about all of this. We can't hear any music. And yet there are no collisions, no bumping, not even any stepping on toes! The only explanation would seem to be some kind of transcendent order of music, many rhythms, all keys at once, a predestined choreography in which each participant meshes with the others. And all move in graceful coordination to produce a beautiful work of art.

If the church, the universal body of believers, could be choreographed, that's the way I think it ideally would appear. Believers have been redeemed "out of every tribe and language and people and nation" (Rev. 5:9). Each one is unique, with a different temperament, personality, character, and physical attributes. Each has a distinctive outlook, philosophy, and perspective. Yet each shares a common salvation in Christ.

This common bond of our Christian faith is nowhere so clearly revealed as when we meet with fellow believers in foreign countries. Several years ago my wife and I had the opportunity to fellowship with believers in Germany, in Austria, in France, and in Italy. Though we sometimes had trouble understanding each other, we enjoyed a communion that went beyond the language barrier. This is possible because all Christians everywhere are citizens of heaven, as Paul writes in Philippians 3:20.

THE HARMONIOUS EXERCISE OF SPIRITUAL GIFTS DEPENDS ON SELF-DISCIPLINE

God has given believers in every local congregation diversified abilities, talents, and gifts. When we are self-disciplined enough to use them, the needs of every member will be met. Some say there are five *speaking* gifts (prophecy or "forth-telling" the Word of God, teaching, exhortation, knowledge, and wisdom) and seven *serving* gifts (faith, discernment, helps, showing mercy, administration, governing, and giving), according to Ephesians 4 and Romans 12. In the Romans passage there are seven gifts in two categories: *expounding* gifts (prophecy, ministry, teaching, exhortation) and *expanding* gifts (giving, ruling, showing mercy).

Suppose I have the gift of helps. If I am so unorganized that I'm never available, how can I exercise my gift? Or suppose I have the gift of exhortation. If my emotions are so undisciplined that I am frequently depressed, how can I edify others? Other members of the body of Christ will suffer if you and I do not exercise our gifts in a disciplined way.

When we *are* self-disciplined, we complement each other; we enhance the spiritual lives of others. And when we act in spiritual sync, we perform a beautiful choreography of praise to our God!

At the end of his fantasy novel *Perelandra,* C. S. Lewis describes a similar performance of praise to God—"The Great Dance" of the redeemed.

> In the plan of the Great Dance, plans without number interlock, and each movement becomes in its season the breaking into flower of the whole design to which all else had been directed. Thus each is equally at the center and none are there by being equals, but

some by giving place and some by receiving it, the small things by their smallness and the great by their greatness, and all the patterns linked and looped together by the unions of a kneeling with a sceptered love. . . .

There seems to be no plan because it is all plan: there seems to be no centre because it is all centre. . . .

The Great Dance seemed to be woven out of the intertwining undulation of many cords or beads of light, leaping over and under one another and mutually embraced in arabesques and flower-like subtleties. Each figure . . . became the master-figure or focus of the whole spectacle, by means of which his eye disentangled all else and brought it into unity.

The emphasis is on unity and union, on intertwining and interlocking, on linking and looping, on giving and receiving, on plan, design, and pattern. Such graceful movement is possible only if each participant is in sync—and such synchronization is possible only through the utmost of self-control.

But how can each individual be in such harmonious control with no audible music to follow—and, in fact, with the harsh Muzak of this worldly system blaring? In the answer to that question lies the great mystery and power of the church—and the secret of self-discipline: *Christ in us* (Col. 1:27). The key to harmony in the church is individual self-control, and the key to individual self-control is to be controlled by the Spirit of Christ.

We've probably all heard that rather misleading, hackneyed statement, "A church is only as strong as its weakest member." This would be true, of course, if the church were a simple chain. Perhaps a more valid statement would be: "The harmonious functioning of the church lies in direct proportion to the self-discipline of its individual members." Self-discipline, I believe, is the key that unlocks the treasure chest of spiritual gifts and releases them to function for the benefit of every believer.

Another "chestnut" we've probably all heard is this one: "If every member were just like me, what kind of church would my church be?" Permit me to reword it as follows: "If every member were as self-disciplined (or as undisciplined) as I am, what kind of a church would my church be?" Would the services ever begin on time? Would the songs and sermons be well prepared and effectively presented? Would the outreach to the community be effective and consistent? Would anyone ever be led to Christ? Would believers be built up in the faith? Would the needy be cared for? Would the sick be visited and ministered to? In other words, would the work of God be done if it depended upon the extent of *my* self-discipline?

Just as self-discipline needs to be instilled in every member of the family, so it needs to be instilled into every member of the family of God. Each of the means of instilling self-discipline in children applies as well to the family of God and specifically to any local body of believers.

It's significant that the scriptural requirement for spiritual leadership in the church is the effective discipline of one's own family—and before that his own self-discipline. A spiritual leader in the church "must be circumspect and temperate and self-controlled," Paul wrote to Timothy. He must "lead an orderly, disciplined life. . . . He must rule his own household well, keeping his children under control, with true dignity, commanding their respect in every way and keeping them respectful. For if a man does not know how to rule his own household, how is he to take care of the church of God?" (1 Tim. 3:2, 4–5 AMPLIFIED).

Note God's order of prerequisites: self-discipline is essential to family discipline, and effective family discipline (which instills self-discipline) is essential to discipline in the body of Christ. The health of our homes and churches depends upon the self-discipline of individual believers, particularly of spiritual leaders.

For lack of self-discipline in an individual life, a home can be lost. For lack of self-discipline in a home, a church can be lost. And for lack of self-discipline in a church, a community can be lost. And all for the lack of individual and corporate self-discipline!

Paul prayed that there would be "glory in the church" (Eph. 3:21). He makes it clear in the next chapter that this desired glory results from unity in diversity. He specifies seven unities—one body, one Spirit, one hope, one Lord, one faith, one baptism, one God and Father of all (vv. 4–6). Note that we are not commanded to *establish* unity, just to *maintain* it. Unity comes as a matter of course when individual believers manifest humility, gentleness, and loving patience in bearing with one another's faults (v. 2). Unity is maintained when individual believers are self-disciplined.

THE CHURCH IS A BODY:
ITS MEMBERS NEED COORDINATION

The most common metaphor used in the Scripture to characterize the church is that of a living body. The body consists of many different parts, each with its own unique function. "There are certainly many limbs and organs, but a single body" (1 Cor. 12:20 AMPLIFIED).

Just as there are feet and hands, ears and eyes and noses in our physical bodies, so there are different kinds of people with different functions in the church. Some individuals are skillful at working with their hands. They may be mechanics or carpenters or electricians or construction workers. They can perform a valuable service within a local congregation. Others may not be able to drive a nail straight, repair a broken bus, or lay a foundation, but they may be skillful in visiting people, in establishing a bus route, or in teaching a Sunday school class.

Paul says that the eye cannot say to the hand, "I don't need you"; neither can the head say to the feet, "I don't need you" (1 Cor. 12:21). Similarly, in the body of Christ, no Christian is unimportant. The highly educated professional man cannot say to the less-educated manual laborer, "We don't need you"— nor vice-versa. We all need each other, and God intends it so.

Suppose my foot rebelled one day and said something like this: "Why am I always the one to hit the hard pavement? Look at those lily-white hands up there, just hanging around, dawdling all day and never getting dirty. I think this body ought to do a flip and let those hands do the walking for awhile!" Or suppose one morning when I get up and prepare for a flight to Denver, one foot insists on going to San Francisco instead! Or suppose my foot or arm insists on staying awake and active when the rest of the body craves sleep, or sleeping when the rest of the body is awake and moving.

Can you imagine an ear rebelling and saying, "I'm not appreciated for what I do, not like those blue eyes in the favored position in front! All I'm good for is holding the temple of these glasses so those eyes can see! I'd like to let the glasses fall and break. Then maybe I'd be appreciated around here!" Silly, you say? Yes it is. But is it really any sillier than a member of the body of Christ resenting a fellow believer because he or she may have a more conspicuous position or may receive more attention?

There is a dreaded physical affliction in which individual cells of the body are in undisciplined rebellion, attacking healthy cells. It's called carcinoma, more commonly known as *cancer*. Paul warned Timothy that undisciplined, unholy talk "will spread like a cancer" (2 Tim. 2:17 BECK).

A city or house divided against itself cannot stand, Jesus said (Matt. 12:25). Neither can a body at odds within itself survive for very long.

Lack of self-discipline brings discord, and eventually division, in the body of Christ. Sometimes when its lack leads to conflicts, it becomes necessary for the pastor and spiritual leaders to exercise church discipline on the basis of such passages as Matthew 18:15–17 and 1 Corinthians 5. Paul even spoke of the need to deliver undisciplined members of the church at Corinth to Satan for the destruction of the flesh in order to prevent further spiritual disorder. Failure to exercise this kind of church discipline today has resulted in the splitting of numerous churches, but the original source of the problem is lack of self-discipline.

God has made ample provision for unity and harmonious functioning of every part and the whole. "God has so adjusted (mingled, harmonized and subtly proportioned the parts of the whole) body, giving the greater honor and richer endowment to the inferior parts which lack (apparent importance)" (1 Cor. 12:24 AMPLIFIED). This is why Paul commanded, as part of our spiritual/relational discipline, that we "give preference to one another in honor" (Rom. 12:10 NASB).

How many of us can honestly say we give preference to our brothers and sisters? Do we really esteem others better (of more account, more important, superior) than ourselves, as Paul commands us to do in Romans 12:10? Only when we are fully under God's control will we "stop looking after our own interests only [and] practice looking out for the interests of others too" (Phil. 2:4 WILLIAMS).

Do you and I manifest the kind of self-discipline that puts the needs and interests of fellow believers before our own "rights" and desires? I can recall how my father, on the farm in Illinois, often illustrated this unselfish attitude. Farmers then worked together to harvest their oats and corn. My father had one of the few threshing machines in the area, so he would spend several months in the late summer and fall going from neighboring farm to farm threshing the oats. Sometimes he was so busy harvesting the neighbor's grain that his own crop would produce a lower yield because of rains or hail or windstorms.

God's prescription for a smoothly functioning body appears in one of the passages that discusses spiritual gifts—Ephesians 4. The secret lies in each member being under the control of the head, which is Christ. "Under his control all the different parts of the body fit together, and the whole body is held together by every joint with which it is provided" (v. 16 GNB). Or as the Weymouth translation puts it, the body "grows by the aid of every contributory ligament." Just as the human brain controls each part of the physical body, so Jesus as Lord controls each part of the body of believers. Trouble arises when any member refuses the control of the Spirit of Christ.

The natural tendency is to seize control ourselves rather than to let the Spirit control us. Ironically, as we have seen, this is not genuine self-control at all. Our old sinful nature is allied with Satan, so whenever that "self" assumes control, essentially the god of this world is in control. The Scripture clearly indicates that there are only two forms of control: we can walk after the flesh, with *Satan* in control; or we can walk after the Spirit, with *God* in control (Rom. 7:1). It's one or the other.

We can walk after the Spirit only by being filled with the Spirit of God in obedience to Ephesians 5:18. This is part of the spiritual self-discipline discussed in Chapter Seven. Further, it involves mental self-discipline. Paul urges the Ephesian believers to "be renewed in the spirit of your mind" (4:23). And it involves discipline of the emotions and tongue: "Wherefore putting away lying, speak every man truth with his neighbor" (Eph. 4:25 KJV).

We are "intimately related to one another in Christ" (Eph. 4:25 PHILLIPS). God makes a harmony in the body when the members of the body mutually care for one another. Each individual believer's attention should be directed outward to the needs of others.

In rebuking the Corinthian believers for their undisciplined disorders at the Lord's Table (carnality, drunkenness, division), Paul urged them to examine themselves and judge themselves in order to escape divine chastisement. Specifically, he said, we partake unworthily if we do not discern the Lord's body (1 Cor. 11:29). His primary meaning is that we must recognize with due appreciation the Lord's broken body, symbolized by the bread. But surely a secondary meaning is the necessity to discern, recognize, appreciate, and be concerned about fellow believers who make up the visible body of Christ. Such a view is supported by subsequent chapters (12–14), which discuss the body of Christ. Further, in the preceding chapter, Paul writes, "We being many, are one bread, and one body" (1 Cor. 10:17 KJV). William Barclay's translation of the clause in 11:29 lends further support to such a reading: "He does not realize that the church is the body of Christ, and therefore a unity with no divisions."

How does discerning the body relate to corporate self-discipline? Self-discipline goes much further and deeper than recognizing and appreciating our brothers and sisters. The body of Christ must manifest what the physical body does—the principles of *compensation*. About six months ago I sprained my ankle while jogging, aggravating an old injury I received in a college wrestling class. The ankle became severely swollen, black-and-blue, and painful to walk on. Now imagine my other ankle reacting as some members of the body of Christ react when a fellow believer is hurting or is taken in a fault. Not only would the healthy ankle likely resent having to carry more of the load, it might even try to kick the hurt ankle, getting in a few good ones when nobody is looking!

Fortunately, our physical bodies don't operate that way. Whenever one member or organ is hurt or incapacitated, the rest of the body works harder to compensate. Loss of eyesight usually results in a keener sense of hearing. An infection in one part of the body, even if it's only the little toe, affects the entire system. White blood corpuscles are produced in bone marrow throughout the body to fight the infection.

This principle of compensation should also be true in the spiritual body when a fellow believer's self-discipline breaks down. Paul wrote, "Brothers, if someone is caught [overtaken] in a sin, you who are spiritual [spiritually self-disciplined], should restore him gently [emotional self-discipline]. But watch yourself [mental self-discipline], or you also may be tempted" (Gal. 6:1). How do you and I react when a Christian brother or sister makes a false step? An impulsive, undisciplined condemning response could well drive that one farther from self-disciplined living to the point where only severe divine discipline can bring reclamation. On the other hand, a gentle, loving reaction can restore that believer to fellowship and encourage him in his own self-discipline.

THE CHURCH IS A BUILDING:
ITS STONES NEED TO BE BUILT UP

The unity of self-disciplined believers serving the Lord together is also compared to a well-designed, well-constructed building. "You are a structure of God's design," Paul told the Corinthian believers (1 Cor. 3:9 KNOX). And to the believers at Ephesus, he wrote: "You are a building which has been reared on the foundation of the apostles and prophets" (2:20 WEYMOUTH).

Each of the persons of the Trinity has a distinct part in this spiritual building. Those who comprise the building are of God's household. Jesus Christ is the chief cornerstone. And the Holy Spirit is both the instrument of its construction and the inhabitant of the building (Eph. 2:19–22).

The success of any building project depends upon at least four factors. First, there must be a superlative design, a set of blueprints. This is the work of God the Father, for we are *God's* building.

Second, there must be a strong foundation. God the Son, the founding-stone, provides this requirement. "No one can lay any foundation other than the one already laid, which is Jesus Christ" (1 Cor. 3:11). The chief cornerstone provides the model to which all the other stones must conform.

Third, there must be a building superintendent who chooses the right materials and directs the construction. This function is performed by the Holy Spirit, who, in His sovereignty, calls out a people for His name and draws them to the Cross.

A fourth essential element in construction is the builders themselves. Have you ever noticed that we as believers are both the *stones* and the *builders?* Peter says we are like "living stones" rejected by men but chosen by God. Then he admonishes us to let ourselves be used in building the spiritual house (1 Peter 2:5). Williams has translated this verse with a strong reflexive mode: "Keep on building yourselves up, as living stones, unto a spiritual house."

It is God's plan that individual believers edify other believers and, in turn, be edified by them. To edify means to build up, establish, improve, contribute to the advancement of a person's spiritual condition, to instruct or enlighten.

A major component of edification is self-discipline, both of the edifier and of the one being edified. Have you ever noticed that almost every time edification is mentioned in the Scripture it's associated with self-discipline? Paul says that spiritual gifts are given explicitly "for the edifying of the body of Christ" (Eph. 4:12 KJV). In fact, all things are to be done for the purpose of edifying, Paul says twice (1 Cor. 14:26 and 2 Cor. 12:19). In other words, a criterion for determining our behavior is: Will it build up my brothers and sisters in Christ? Will this act hinder rather than help fellow believers?

If we are spiritually self-disciplined, we will graciously curb what we might be inclined to do or say if the act or remark might damage another "living stone." Erwin W. Lutzer, in his book *How in This World Can I Be Holy?*, notes that "we should gladly conform to certain disciplines rather than hinder our brother's spiritual welfare." For example, suppose my friend, recently converted and a babe in Christ, has strong convictions against Sunday sports because he feels Sunday should be a day of rest, worship, and meditation on the Scriptures. Shouldn't I exercise self-discipline in forgoing Sunday golf or watching the Super Bowl game if my engaging in these activities would offend or hinder my brother?

Here is where individual self-discipline can lead to corporate self-discipline. "We who are strong ought to bear with the failings of the weak," Paul says, "and not to please ourselves. Each of us should please his neighbor, for his good, to build him up" (Rom. 15:1–2). This is a plea for Christian patience, an attribute of self-discipline. We are to be *forbearing*—rather than the bears we so often seem to be. We are to *bear with* the weaknesses of our brothers and sisters, not insisting on having our own ways. The strong, self-disciplined believer retains his spiritual liberty in Christ ("all things are lawful for me"), though he does not do everything he may have a "right" to do ("all things edify not"). A believer who insists on doing everything he feels he is at liberty to do, not only lacks self-discipline but he is unlike Christ, who did not please Himself (Rom. 15:3). And in living to please himself, such a person does not build up fellow believers and encourage *them* in self-discipline.

A disciplined tongue, for example, will speak positive words of encouragement, building up rather than tearing down. "Do not let any unwholesome talk come out of your mouth," Paul advises, "but only what is helpful for building others up according to their needs . . ." (Eph. 4:29). The key word in this verse, translated "corrupt communication" in the King James Version, is very forceful, carrying the image of a rotten, putrid fish. Have you ever been walking along a beautiful lake or river and come across dead fish that someone has left? It's hard to imagine a more unpleasant smell. God says that's what our undisciplined, unwholesome talk is like.

But when our tongues are self-disciplined and our speech is sprinkled with the salt of grace (Col. 4:6), we build others up by "ministering grace to those who hear" (Eph. 4:29 KJV). In his farewell address to the Ephesian elders, Paul commended them "to God and to the word of his grace, which is able to build you up" (Acts 20:29 KJV). If we are self-disciplined, we will speak words of grace. Gracious words will minister grace to those who hear. Grace ministered to others builds them up. And to be built up means, among other things, becoming more self-disciplined.

Grace, that divinely imparted ability to transform unpleasing circumstances into pleasing ones, is both a cause and an effect of self-discipline, which, in turn, produces more self-discipline. One of the glorious truths of the Christian experience is the *contagion* (in a positive sense—from a Latin word meaning "a touching") of self-discipline. If the *lack* of self-discipline in a few spreads to many in the group, the self-disciplined living of a few individuals can spread to others in a local assembly. Which of us has not been encouraged and strengthened in our self-disciplined living by fellowship with other believers? In my own case, attending a weekly men's prayer breakfast and a weekly Bible study with Christian colleagues has caused me to be more disciplined in my own private Bible study and prayer.

Perhaps praying together, studying God's Word together, and sharing concerns with other Christians has built me up most by rubbing off some of the rough edges. Whenever you get two "living stones"—or four, six, eight, or more—close together, the rough edges begin to show up. Oh, we all have them. Rough edges like self-centeredness, egotism, covetousness, greed, envy, sloth, a critical attitude, cynicism, a sharp tongue, and others. Can you imagine trying to build a smooth, straight, level building with rough, uneven, jagged stones? Well, that's what God has to work with—you and me. But He isn't finished with us yet! He's putting us with other stones so those rough edges can be rubbed smooth. Or maybe they have to be chiseled into shape. The chiseling and abrasion aren't pleasant, but they are necessary.

Have you ever wondered why that surly neighbor has to live on *your* street? Maybe you have some rough edges God wants removed so you'll be a smooth stone for His building. Have you wondered why you have to work with that unpleasant person who is so insensitive and thoughtless in his remarks? Maybe God is using that trying situation to smooth some rough edges on your character. Are you bothered by someone at church you always seem to clash with? Let the grace of God smooth out those rough edges and, with the mortar of His love, fashion you as a part of His glorious building.

But the smoothing of rough edges must come as part of the process of loving acceptance and fellowship, not from our selecting a stone-in-the-rough and resolving to smooth it out to conform to *our* image of what the person should be like. Such efforts, sincere though they may be, are ordinarily misguided manifestations of our *own* lack of self-discipline, itself perhaps one of our rough edges. Be wary of setting out to change someone else! You might get changed yourself!

For example, in my efforts at self-discipline, I have made a special effort to be on time, preferably allowing fifteen or twenty minutes leeway in case of unforeseen delays. I was becoming increasingly more and more frustrated when my family wasn't ready to leave for Sunday school and church at the crack of 9:30. There was my wife, bustling around trying to get dressed, trying to peel potatoes and get the roast on for dinner, trying to supervise the dressing of two boys—while I walked through the house announcing, "Four minutes till blast off!" The rough edge, I realized, was largely my own. I was trying to be so self-disciplined in my promptness that I was becoming impatient and thoughtless.

Things went considerably better after our family came to this agreement one Saturday night: "Tomorrow we'll leave for church at 9:30. We'll have to get up 30 minutes earlier. Breakfast at 8:45. You guys will have to be up and dressed by then. Dad will peel the potatoes and get the roast on so that mom can do her hair."

A second word of caution: just as we can't program God's patterns, neither can we program His people and purposes. Sometimes we edify and enhance the self-discipline of individuals we may think we have little or no effect upon. Several weeks ago I received a call from a man who used to attend the same church I do, but I hadn't seen him for three or four years. He expressed appreciation for my teaching and then told me something of which I had never been aware. About four years previously he had overheard a verbal exchange in which I had reacted graciously under some very trying and provocative circumstances. Apparently that brief reaction, which by the grace of God was a self-disciplined one, had made a lasting impression on this man and had contributed to his own spiritual growth.

Similarly, we are sometimes edified by and learn lessons from the least likely individuals. Most of the people who have influenced my Christian growth haven't been flashy, sophisticated ones in the limelight. Rather, they've mostly been simple people, many of them shy and retiring. But they have it all together for the Lord and are faithfully serving Him. No flashing lights, no fanfare, no applause from the crowd. But God doesn't require those things. You don't even necessarily need a mortarboard to build up the temple of the Lord!

THE CHURCH IS A BRIDE: SHE NEEDS TO BE ADORNED FOR THE BRIDEGROOM

Every true believer from Pentecost to the first resurrection comprises the bride of Christ. The preparation and adornment of the bride for the Bridegroom demands the utmost in individual and corporate self-discipline.

The eastern pattern of marriage in Bible times involved three separate stages of the wedding. The Scripture speaks of all three, draws analogies with the Christian life, and suggests implications about self-discipline. First, there was the espousal or betrothal, a legally binding mutual commitment. In the spiritual realm, when we are converted, we are espoused to Christ. Paul told the Corinthian believers, "I promised you to one husband, so that I might present you as a pure virgin to him" (2 Cor. 11:2). The emphasis here is on chastity. The bride presented to Christ must be pure and without blemish.

The applicability of self-discipline should be obvious: component parts of the bride should help each other discipline themselves unto godliness. For too long we've assumed godly living to be simply an individual matter: you live your life as you will, and I'll live mine. That's the way of the world. But it's not the intended way of life in the body, the building, and the bride.

John Donne, the seventeenth-century English poet, expressed this interrelation in one of his meditations from *Devotions Upon Emergent Occasions:* "No man is an island, entire of itself; every man is a piece of the continent, a part of the main. If a clod be washed away by the sea, Europe is the less, as well as if a promontory were, as well as if a manor of thy friend's or of thine own were: any man's death diminishes me, because I am involved in mankind, and therefore never send to know for whom the bell tolls: it tolls for thee." We might well paraphrase Donne's words as follows: "Any brother's defeat, any sister's fall, diminishes me, because I am involved in the bride of Christ."

The effect of this involvement was borne out recently in a small Bible study group. When one man told how he was sorely tempted every time he went past an "adult" bookstore, each member of the group, sincerely bearing the man's concern, interceded on his behalf. God used this devotion and encouragement to give the man glorious victory over the besetting temptation.

A second emphasis in our spiritual betrothal to Christ is subjection. In Ephesians 5, Paul says that wives are to be submissive to their husbands just as the church is submissive to Christ. Again the relation to corporate self-discipline should be obvious. The church as a whole is submissive to Christ only as individual members are. And this submission of individuals to Christ entails, as Paul says earlier in the same chapter, "submitting [ourselves] one to another in the fear of God" (v. 21 KJV). We willingly yield our rights in love. And that requires some self-discipline!

A second stage of the eastern wedding was the coming of the bridegroom, attended by friends and musicians, to the bride's house. He would there receive her from her parents and take her to his own house. The spiritual parallel is the second coming of Christ to rapture the church.

The apostle John describes this glorious event as he saw it in his Mt. Patmos vision. "The wedding of the Lamb has come, and his bride has made herself ready" (Rev. 19:7). Note the bride's meticulous preparation of adornment. And note that the bride is preparing *herself*. The bride, John says further, was given in fine radiant linen—bright and white (v. 8).

Psalm 45, a beautiful bridal song, describes her. She is glorious. Her clothing is interwoven with gold. Wearing raiment of needlework, she is brought unto the king. The wrought gold, beautiful tracery resulting from the hammer and tremendous heat, perhaps suggests the discipline of adversity and suffering. The garment of fine needlework may represent a life of devoted service. But it's John who tells us what the bride's exquisite garment symbolizes: "The fine linen is (signifies, represents) the righteousness—the upright, just and godly living (deeds, conduct) and right standing with God—of the saints" (Rev. 19:8 AMPLIFIED).

It's our responsibility as part of the bride of Christ to prepare for the Bridegroom's coming not only by hastening that day through our evangelistic efforts but also by encouraging each other in disciplined, godly living. That's our bridal adornment. There's nothing that motivates disciplined, godly living like a reminder of the Lord's imminent return. That's what John says: "Everyone who has this hope before him purifies himself, as Christ is pure" (1 John 3:3 NEB). By keeping this hope before us, reminding each other of the Lord's soon return, we can enhance the corporate self-discipline of the bride. By so doing, we can be obedient to the command to "watch and be sober-minded" (1 Thess. 5:6 KJV), or, as the *Twentieth Century New Testament* puts it, "be watchful and self-controlled." The tragic results of being unprepared, of failing to watch and be self-disciplined, are clearly shown in the Parable of the Five Foolish Virgins (Matt. 25).

When was the last time you and I comforted (from the Latin meaning "to strengthen much") a brother or sister with a reminder that Jesus is coming soon? In 1 Thessalonians 4:18 we are commanded to comfort each other in this manner. When did we last encourage another and build another up with the promise of Christ's return? We are commanded, "Comfort yourselves together, and edify one another" in the light of the Lord's return (1 Thess. 5:11 KJV). This form of exhortation can generate corporate self-discipline as perhaps nothing else can.

In Revelation 19 the apostle John also refers to the third stage of the eastern marriage: the wedding feast. After the bridegroom, bride, and accompanying friends and musicians returned to the bridegroom's house, other friends joined the joyful festivities. "They are led in with joy and gladness; they enter the palace of the king" (Ps. 45:15). The eating and merrymaking usually continued for a week or more. The spiritual parallel is Christ's return to the earth with His bride to establish His thousand-year reign on earth.

Further implications for self-discipline lie in the fourfold charge to the bride as recorded in Psalm 45: "Listen, O daughter, consider and give ear: *Forget* your people and your father's house" (v. 10). There really are two things we who make up the bride of Christ are to do. We are to focus our whole beings upon the Bridegroom, and we are to forget the old fleshly, self-centered life.

This same twofold, positive-negative practice is reflected in Paul's admonition, "Set your minds on things above, not on earthly things" (Col. 3:2). This high ideal is possible to achieve only if we have died to the world and have a new life in Christ (v. 3). We can help each other set our minds on Christ—and keep them set on Him. Sometimes just a word—especially if it's God's Word—will help someone refocus his or her mind on Christ. It might be a single word like "Maranatha," "The Lord is coming." Or it might be a pat on the back and an assurance such as, "God loves you, and I love you."

The "good word" reinforcement of self-discipline might be an appropriate promise from Scripture we share with a brother or sister. The one that has helped me perhaps more than any other single verse, especially in my sometimes frustrating efforts at self-discipline, is this one: "The Lord is at hand" (Phil. 4:5 KJV). The promise has a dual application. Not only does it mean that the Lord's second coming is near; it also means that He is ever-present, readily available, easily accessible whenever we need Him! And is there ever a time when we don't need Him?

Without Him, our lives are undisciplined and out of control. Without the head, the body is simply an uncoordinated bag of bones. Without the chief cornerstone, the building is simply an amorphous pile of stones. Without the Bridegroom, the bride is simply an incomplete entity, without fulfillment or even a reason for existence. But because the Lord *is* at hand, our moderation, our forbearance, our sweet reasonableness, our self-discipline can be known unto and among everyone.

The Lord is at hand to help you become more self-disciplined: spiritually, mentally, emotionally, physically, verbally, and in terms of time management. Why not begin, with God's help, your own Project for Achieving Self-Discipline? Start with a prayer of commitment, yielding control to the Spirit of God in obedience to Ephesians 5:18. Renew the commitment each day. Keep a daily journal of your transactions and progress. In six weeks retake the inventory questionnaire in the introduction of this book and see God work in your life.

There's nothing quite like the testimony of the lives of believers who have it all together, who are firmly in the driver's seat, who are individually and corporately self-disciplined! Your life and mind can be such a one, for "God is the Energizer within you, so as to will and to work for His delight" (Phil. 2:13).

For Further Reading

Chapter 6

"Discerning the Devil's Deductions," *Christianity Today*, 10
  November 1972.
"The Devil's Electric Carrot," *Christianity Today*, 16 February
  1973.
"13 Ways to Beat the Devil," *Eternity*, May 1972.
"The Grammar of Grace," *Christianity Today*, 15 January 1973.
"Where Has the Charisma Gone?" *Christianity Today*, 30 Au-
  gust 1974.

Chapter 8

"Sneaky Stimuli and How to Resist Them," *Christianity Today*,
  31 January 1975.
A Primer on Meditation: How to Reflect on the Word of God
  (Colorado Springs: Navigators Press, n.d.).